Tony Panozzo's Homegrown Sliced Tomatoes   page 22
Inserts:
Tony Panozzo Farms, Kankakee, IL
Grilled Summer Salad   page 21

A Need to Feed

a cookbook by

Patricia Panozzo

Welcome to my home!

Come in...

Sit down.

Here, eat.

Have some more.

Eat.

There's plenty.

Enjoy!

With much love,
Patty

This is dedicated to my "Nona next door" and "Grandma down the road",
whose knowledge of cooking inspired me to write this cookbook.
Watching them in the kitchen was like watching a beautiful dance.
They live on in their many recipes passed down from generation to generation.
What a beautiful gift you have given us.
Thank you God for giving them to me.

To my Dad and Mom, your love and support are never ending.

To my sister, Marie, whose heart is as big as the world, and kindness equally
as vast. I have learned so much from you and treasure you deeply.

To my sister, Lorena, that you have found peace in your afterlife.

To my brother, Alex,
"You are my sunshine.... you'll never know dear, how much I love you".
You are all things precious to me.

To Michael Wood, my spiritual partner and mentor. I love you always.

To my dear friend Kathleen Kennedy Shepherd.
I could not have done this without you.

To Mary Ann DeBoo, my very best friend, ever.
Now, gone to a higher place. I miss you , Mare........a lot.
You too, Sage.
Bride O'Shaughnessy, you are my soul sister.
Tony Lott, you are my brother.

And all my precious friends, none of which I ever take for granted.
I love all you guys, so much!

Patty

Copyright 1999 by Patricia Panozzo:
Panozzo, Inc., P.O. Box 6, Lakeside, MI 49116

Cookbooks available at:

Toll free   877 RECIPE 2
                 (877 732-4732)

www.aneedtofeed.com

Also at: 219 926-1551
                 616 469-4364

ISBN 0-9623704-0-1

Cover by Patricia Panozzo

Technical and art direction by: Editing assistance by:
Design Concepts   Rose Panozzo
Kathleen Kennedy Shepherd   Kankakee
815 933.1589   IL
designc@keynet.net   A special thanks to my Mom for her help.

Color photos by: Photo stylist assistance:
THE f /STOPS HERE   Shirley Myers
Richard E. Hellyer   smyers@mich.com
616 426.3102

Stoneware by: Italian ceramic platters from:
Bret Bortner Design   Decora Euroimport Ltd.
wabi/sabi 800 551.3701   800 200.0554

Accessories, gourmet foods and P. Panozzo's cookbooks, available at:
Panozzo's Pantry in the Schoolhouse Shop
278 E. 1500 N.
Chesterton, IN   46304
219 926.1551

Printed by: Bookmasters, Inc
Mansfield, OH 800 537-6727
Special thanks to: Alan Worley

CONTENTS

SALADS
Main

You can create a new salad by just turning a section of each page. What a variety!

1

Cut along these lines on the following pages.

Filler

And practical too!
You can effortlessly tailor a recipe to fit your tastes or dietary needs.

2

Cut along these lines on the following pages.

Dressing

So, make your life easier with just a turn of a page. Have some fun and flip through it! You will amaze yourself and your taste buds!

3

These serve 4-6 as a main course or 6-8 as a side dish.
The salads also work well with just sections 2 and 3 for vegetarian salads.

CHICKEN, TURKEY or DUCK

Add to a mixing bowl:

2-3 lbs.	CHICKEN, TURKEY or DUCK - skinless, boneless cooked

1

Saute, grill, roast or bake.
Cut into strips or chunks.
Optional: Before cooking, pick a dressing from #3 and marinate for 15 minutes or longer.
Can be marinated overnight.

- ✂
Cut along these lines.

SUGAR SNAP PEAS

Add:

3 cups	SUGAR SNAP PEAS, cleaned
1 cup	CHERRY TOMATOES, halved
1 cup	MUSHROOMS, sliced
1/2 cup	CARROTS, grated or julienned
1/2 cup	RED ONION, thinly sliced

2

- ✂
Cut along these lines.

CILANTRO LIME DRESSING

Mix together in small bowl:

1/3 cup	LIME JUICE
1/4 cup	CORN OIL
1/8 cup	WHITE WINE VINEGAR
1/3 cup	Fresh CILANTRO, chopped
1 tbsp.	OLIVE OIL
1 tbsp.	Fresh GINGER, peeled, minced
1 clove	GARLIC, minced
1 tsp.	Grated LIME PEEL
	SALT, PEPPER & Hot Sauce to taste

3

Pour desired amount over 1 & 2 and toss.
Refrigerate remaining dressing.

FISH

Add to mixing bowl:

    2-3 lb.   FISH - cooked

Sauté, grill, roast or bake.
Break up into bite size pieces.
Optional: Before cooking, pick a dressing from #3 and marinate for 15 minutes or longer.
Can be marinated overnight.

1

- ✂ - - - - -

Cut along these lines.

RICE

Add:

    4 cups   RICE, cooked White, Brown and/or Basmati
    1/2 cup   GREEN ONIONS, chopped or Chives, chopped

2

- ✂ - - - - -

Cut along these lines.

THAI DRESSING

Mix together in a small bowl:
    1/4 cup   LIME JUICE
    1/4 cup   SESAME OIL
    1/4 cup   COCONUT MILK
    1/8 cup   SOY SAUCE
    2 tbsps.   PEANUT BUTTER
    1 tbsp.   Fresh GINGER ROOT, peeled & grated
    1 tsp.   CORRIANDER
    1/2 tsp.   CURRY POWDER
                CHILI PEPPERS, SALT & PEPPER to taste

3

Pour desired amount over 1 & 2 and toss.
Refrigerate remaining dressing.

SHELLFISH

Add to a mixing bowl:

4-5 cups   SHELL FISH - cooked
(Oysters, Shrimp, Scallops, Clams - leave whole.
Crab & Lobster - cut up)

1

Sauté or grill.
Optional: Before cooking, pick a dressing from #3 and marinate for 15 minutes or longer.

page 4

✂ - - - - - - - - - - - - - - -
Cut along these lines.

PEAPODS

Add:

4 cups   PEAPODS,
clean & leave whole

Steam until tender.

2

Add:

1 cup   PEANUTS, chopped
1 cup   RED CABBAGE, shredded

page 4

✂ - - - - - - - - - - - - - - -
Cut along these lines.

TERIYAKI DRESSING

Mix together in a small bowl:

1 cup   TERIYAKI SAUCE
1/4 cup   RICE VINEGAR or white vinegar
1/4 cup   Chopped GREEN ONIONS

3

Optional: To make it spicy add, 1/2-1 teaspoon WASBI
Pour desired amount over 1 & 2 and toss.
Refrigerate remaining dressing.

LAMB

Add to mixing bowl:

2-3 lbs.	LAMB - cooked	**1**

Sauté, grill, roast or bake.
Cut up into strips or bite sized pieces.
Optional: Before cooking, pick a dressing from #3 and marinate for 15 minutes or longer.
Can be marinated overnight.

- ✂ - - -
Cut along these lines.

COUSCOUS

Add:

4 cups	COUSCOUS, cooked	**2**
1/2 cup	CARROTS, grated	
1/2 cup	GREEN ONIONS or Chives, chopped	

- ✂ - - -
Cut along these lines.

ROSEMARY DRESSING

Mix together in small bowl:

1/3 cup	OLIVE OIL
1/8 cup	EXTRA VIRGIN OLIVE OIL
1/3 cup	BALSAMIC VINEGAR
1/8 cup	LEMON JUICE
1/8 cup	Grated PARMESAN
1/4 cup	Fresh ROSEMARY, chopped, or 1 tbsp. dried rosemary
1 tsp.	Dried OREGANO
1-2 cloves	GARLIC, minced
	SALT & PEPPER to taste

3

Pour desired amount over 1 & 2 and toss.
Refrigerate remaining dressing.

BEEF or OSTRICH

Add to a mixing bowl:

2-3 lbs.	BEEF, use a tender cut of meat -cooked
	or
	Ostrich - cooked

Sauté, grill, roast or bake.
Slice into strips.
Optional: Before cooking, pick a dressing from #3 and marinate for 15 minutes or longer.
Can be marinated overnight.

1

- -
Cut along these lines.

POTATOES

Add:

4 cups	RED POTATOES, cooked and cut up. Do not peel.
	Do not overcook. Potatoes should be firm and not be mushy.
1 cup	CELERY, cut up
1/2 cup	PARSLEY, chopped
1 small	RED ONION, thinly sliced

2

- -
Cut along these lines.

BASIL DRESSING

Add to a blender:

1/3 cup	OLIVE OIL
1/8 cup	EXTRA VIRGIN OLIVE OIL
1/3 cup	VINEGAR
1/8 cup	LEMON JUICE
1 cup	Fresh BASIL LEAVES
1/4 cup	PARMESAN, grated
1-3 cloves	GARLIC
	SALT & PEPPER to taste

3

Blend until smooth.
Pour desired amount over 1 & 2 and toss.
Refrigerate remaining dressing.

VEGGIES

Add to mixing bowl:

    4 cups Cut up VEGETABLES, raw or cooked

To make the salad interesting and visually appealing, select vegetables that vary in color and texture
Or, in the real world: just clean out the vegetable drawer!

If you are using cooked vegetables, sauté, grill, roast or steam them.
Optional: Pick a dressing from #3 and marinate for 15 minutes or longer.

1

page 7

- ✂ - - -

Cut along these lines.

PASTA

Add:

12-16 oz.	Bag of PASTA, cooked al dente, drained & rinsed
	Choose from many colored pastas that come in a variety of shapes and sizes.
1 small	RED ONION, thinly sliced
1/2 cup	Chopped PARSLEY
Optional:	
1/2 cup	Snipped Fresh FENNEL LEAVES

2

page 7

- ✂ - - -

Cut along these lines.

NO FAT DRESSING

Add to a blender:

1/2 cup	ORANGE JUICE CONCENTRATE
1/2 cup	GRAPEFRUIT JUICE
1/3 cup	HONEY
2	KIWIS, peeled and cut up and/or
1/2 cup	Strawberries
2 tbsps.	Fresh MINT LEAVES or 4 tbsps. dry
1/2-1 tsp.	TARRAGON
	SALT & PEPPER to taste

3

Blend until smooth. For a creamy dressing, add 1/2-1 c Non Fat PLAIN Yogurt
Pour desired amount over 1 & 2 and toss.
Refrigerate remaining dressing.

page 7

SALAD GREENS

Fill a good size salad bowl 2/3 full of:

GOURMET SALAD GREENS, washed, drained and torn.

Choose from a varity of salad greens to add interest to the salad.

1

page 8

- -

Cut along these lines.   ✂

BEANS

Add:

4 cups	BEANS, canned or cooked and drained (White, Black, Navy, Pinto, Adzuki, Garbanzo, Pigeon, Cranberry beans or Lentils) You can use a combination of different beans and/or lentils.	
1/2 cup	PARSLEY, chopped	
1	RED PEPPER, sliced	
1 small	RED ONION, thinly sliced	
1-2 cloves	GARLIC, minced	

2

page 8

- -

Cut along these lines.   ✂

ITALIAN DRESSING

Mix together in a small bowl:

1/3 cup	OLIVE OIL
1/8 cup	EXTRA VIRGIN OLIVE OIL
1/3 cup	BALSAMIC VINEGAR
1/4 cup	PARMESAN, grated
2 tsps.	ITALIAN SEASONING (oregano, basil, rosemary, marjoram)
1/2 tsp.	FENNEL SEEDS, crushed SALT & PEPPER to taste

3

Pour desired amount over 1 & 2 and toss.
Refrigerate remaining dressing.

SAUSAGE

Add to a mixing bowl:

2-3 lbs.   SAUSAGE - cooked
(regular, Italian, Chorizo or Turkey)

1

Grill or fry. (It is your option to remove or leave sausage casing.)
Drain on paper towels to remove any excess grease.
Cut up into bite size pieces.

✄

- -

Cut along these lines.

ORZO

Add:

4 cups	ORZO, cooked al dente, drained and rinsed
1/2 cup	Grated CARROTS
1/2 cup	Chopped GREEN ONIONS
	or
	Chopped CHIVES

2

✄

- -

Cut along these lines.

SUNDRIED TOMATO DRESSING

Add to a small sauce pan, over medium heat:

1/4 cup	BALSAMIC VINEGAR
1/4 cup	OLIVE OIL
1/8 cup	EXTRA VIRGIN OLIVE OIL
1/2 cup	SUNDRIED TOMATOES, chopped
1-2 cloves	GARLIC, minced
1/2 tsp.each:	FENNEL, BASIL, & ROSEMARY, dried or fresh
	SALT & PEPPER to taste
1-2 tsp.	SUNDRIED TOMATO PASTE or Tomato Paste

3

Bring to boil, stirring occasionally. SALT adn PEPPER to taste.
Cool before using. Optional, Add a few dashes of HOT SAUCE &
WORCESTERSHIRE SAUCE
Pour desired amounts over 1 & 2 and toss.
Refrigerate remaining dressing.

EGG

Add to mixing bowl:

4 cups   Sliced HARD BOILED EGGS

This one comes in very handy as a post Easter salad.

✂   *1*

— — — — — — — — — — — — — — — — Cut along these lines. — — — — — — — — — — —

JICAMA

Add:

4 cups	JICAMA, grated or julienned
1 cup	CARROTS, grated or julienned
1 small	RED ONION, thinly sliced

Add just before serving:

1/2 cup   PUMKIN SEEDS, toasted & shelled Pumkin

Toss together.

✂   *2*

— — — — — — — — — — — — — — — — Cut along these lines. — — — — — — — — — — —

LEMON DILL DRESSING

Mix together in small bowl or blender:

1/3 cup	LEMON JUICE
1/3 cup	GRAPESEED OIL or Lemon Grapeseed Oil
2 tbsps.	CIDER VINEGAR
4 tbsps. heaping	SOUR CREAM or Plain Yogurt
3 tbsps. heaping	MAYONNAISE or Salad Dressing or dill flavored
2 tsp.	Grated LEMON PEEL
1 tbsp.	DILL WEED, dry or fresh
1/2 tsp.	GINGER, dry or fresh, grated
1-2 tbsps.	SUGAR depending on your tastes of tartness
	SALT & PEPPER to taste

Pour desired amounts over 1 & 2 and toss. Refrigerate remaining dressing.

3

VEAL

Add to a mixing bowl:

     2-3 lbs.   VEAL - cooked

1

Sauté, grill, roast or bake.
Cut up into strips.
Optional: Before cooking, pick a dressing from #3 and marinate for 15 minutes or longer.

Cut along these lines. ✂

POLENTA

Add:

2

    4 cups   POLENTA, cut into cubes
               (See recipe for "Basic Polenta" in "Side Dish" section. Cook and pour into oiled baking dish. Cool and cut up.)
    1 small   RED ONION, thinly sliced
    1/2 cup   PARSLEY, chopped
    1/2 cup   Fresh FENNEL, cut up

Cut along these lines. ✂

FETA-OLIVE DRESSING

Mix together in a small bowl:
     1/3 cup   EXTRA VIRGIN OIL
     1/3 cup   BALSAMIC VINEGAR
     1 cup   Crumbled FETA CHEESE
     2/3 cup   Chopped BLACK or GREEN OLIVES or an OLIVE TAPENADE
     1/2 tsp.   ROSEMARY, dry or 1 tsp. fresh, chopped
     1/2 tsp.   THYME, dry
     1-2 cloves GARLIC, minced
                SALT & PEPPER to taste

3

Pour desired amount over 1 & 2 and toss.
Refrigerate remaining dressing.

Summer, Winter,
Spring or Fall,
there is always a salad that
fits the season.

At Panozzo's Cafe we would
assemble 3 different ones
on a plate and call it a
"Salad Sampler".

It makes a wonderful
luncheon entre garnished
with fresh herbs.

SALADS

FLORIBEAN FRUIT & RICE SALAD

This is a perfect summer pleaser combining the flavors of Florida and the Caribbean. Taste the tropics.

◆◆◆◆◆◆◆◆

Serves 4-8

Add to a large mixing bowl:

4 cups	Cooked RICE - White, brown, or basmati white or brown
2 cups	MANGO, peeled and cut up
2 cups	PINEAPPLE, peeled and cut up
1 cup	PAPAYA, seeded, cut off of rind and cut up
	Cantaloupe can be substituted
1/2 cup	Fresh MINT, chopped and packed down
1/3 cup	Frozen ORANGE JUICE CONCENTRATE, thawed
1/3 cup	LIME JUICE
1/3 cup	SUGAR
1/4 cup	OIL - Canola, Corn, Vegetable or Peanut
	SALT & PEPPER to taste

Note: The fruits will juice up, so have everything cut up and ready.
Drain off any juices that have accumulated. Assemble and mix together a few hours before serving.
Toss until well combined.
Refrigerate until ready to serve.

Toss before serving.

Serve on gourmet lettuce leaves and garnish with flower blossoms.

For added color, sprinkle the salad with some:
BLACK BEANS, cooked or POMEGRANATE SEEDS

NOTE: This summer salad is also great topped with grilled or blackened fish or chicken.

◆◆◆◆◆◆◆◆

TUSCANY KALE & WHITE BEAN SALAD

Traveling around Italy in the region of Tuscany, I found this salad to be a simple pleasure. And in the style of it's origin, just throw it together and it will be wonderful!

◆◆◆◆◆◆◆◆

Wash and steam two or three bunches
of fresh KALE.
Drain, chop and transfer to a wooden salad bowl.

Add:
2 cups cooked WHITE BEANS
or one large can, drained.
1 small RED ONION, thinly sliced.
1-3 cloves GARLIC, minced or sliced

Sprinkle with:
SALT and PEPPER

Drizzle with desired amounts of:
VINEGAR and OLIVE OIL

Serve warm, at room temperature or chilled.

◆◆◆◆◆◆◆◆

*For more color, try adding chopped red peppers and black olives.
Serve with plenty of crusty bread.*

15

PANOZZO'S PANTRY

SPINACH OLIVE PASTA SALAD

With all the beautiful gourmet foods in my shop, I cannot resist putting recipes together using some of these delicious products. The reality of the situation is - the foods are great and if it makes our lives easier, why not! As a lover of olives, Michael Wood gives this his stamp of approval.

Serves 8-10

Cook in plenty of boiling salted water until al dente:

1 bag	"CASTELLANA PASTA, Foglie d'Olivia" (This is a beautiful pasta shaped like olive leaves, flavored with spinach.)

Drain and rinse.

Transfer pasta to a large mixing bowl and add:

1 24 oz. jar	"RAO'S SICILIANA SAUCE" (This is a delicious marinara sauce made with eggplant.)
1 12 oz jar	GARLIC STUFFED OLIVES, sliced "Miss Scarlett's Drunken Garlic Stuffed Olives"
1/3 cup	OLIVE JUICE from the garlic stuffed olives
1 small jar	BLACK GOURMET OLIVES, cut up
1 bag	Fresh SPINACH, sliced (reserve some leaves for garnish)
1	RED PEPPER, sliced
1 medium	VIDALIA or RED ONION, thinly sliced
1/2 cup	PARSLEY, chopped
1/2 cup	EXTRA VIRGIN OLIVE OIL
1/2 cup	BALSAMIC VINEGAR
2-4 tbsps.	ITALIAN SEASONING (oregano, basil, rosemary, marjoram, etc.) or 1 cup fresh mixed chopped herbs
	SALT & PEPPER to taste

Toss well and adjust seasonings to suit your tastes.

Garnish with whole olives and spinach leaves.

16

SOUTHWEST SALAD
POTATO - GREEN BEAN

This is a potato salad compared to none. Distinct and delicious.

◆◆◆◆◆◆◆◆

Serves 4-8

Cut up enough RED POTATOES to equal 4 cups.
> Cut into bite size chunks, leaving on skins.
> Boil until barely cooked. Do not over cook.
> Drain.

Cut up enough GREEN BEANS to equal 4 cups.
> Clean and cut into halves.
> Steam until barely cooked. They should have good color and be crisp.
> Drain.

To a large mixing bowl add:
> The boiled & drained POTATOES
>
> The steamed & drained GREEN BEANS
>
> | 2 cups | RED PEPPER - sliced |
> | 1 cup | RED ONION - sliced |
> | 1 cup | Fresh CILANTRO - chopped |
> | 1/2 cup | OIL, Canola, Vegetable, or Corn |
> | 2/3 cup | LIME JUICE |
> | 1/3 cup | ORANGE JUICE |
> | 1-2 | Fresh JALAPENOS, seeded & chopped |
> | 1 tbsp. | Grated LIME PEEL |
> | 1 tsp. | Grated ORANGE PEEL |
> | 1/2 tsp. | CUMIN |
> | | SALT & PEPPER to taste |

Toss until well combined.
Transfer to a serving bowl.
Serve at room temperature or chilled. Toss before serving.

◆◆◆◆◆◆◆◆

Garnish with sliced red pepper rings.

17

ROASTED POTATO OLIVE SALAD

The most important part of this salad is to roast new potatoes with a muffalata olive salad. After that, add whatever suits your tastes is fine.

❖❖❖❖❖❖❖❖

Serves 6-8

Add to a large mixing bowl:

4 lbs.	New RED POTATOES, cut into cubes or wedges
1 cup	Chopped OLIVE SALAD (Muffalata spread) or use marinated mixed chopped olives - using the liquid.
	SALT & PEPPER to taste

Toss together.

Lay potato mixture out on 1 or 2 baking sheets, so potatoes are in one layer.

Bake in preheated 400° F. oven for 30-40 minutes until tender and easily pierced with a fork.

These are delicious out of the oven as a hot side dish. So, if you can resist eating them now, we'll go on to finish the salad.

Transfer the potatoes to a large mixing bowl and add:

1 medium	RED ONION, thinly sliced
1 cup	PARSLEY, (flat or curly) chopped
1 more cup	Chopped OLIVE SALAD
1 cup	Toasted PINE NUTS - optional (celery gives a nice crunch too)

Toss until well combined.

Drizzle with your favorite:

OLIVE OIL

BALSAMIC VINEGAR

Optional: Sprinkle with:

Grated CHEESE

1-2 tbsps.	Fresh ROSEMARY, chopped

Serve warm, at room temperature or cold.

❖❖❖❖❖❖❖❖

Like anchovies? Mash some of those up and toss in. Roasted garlic too!
Dot with fresh mozzerella or goat cheese and cherry tomatoes.

PRINCE RICOTTA POTATO SALAD

Lowfat, creamy and studded with dried cherries, sets it apart from all others. This is an original by John Prince, a maestro of food and music.

A perfect salad for Easter or Mother's Day!

Serves 4-8

Cut up enough RED POTATOES to equal 8 cups.

Cut into bite size chunks, leaving on skins.

Boil until a little overcooked but not mushy.
Drain.

Add to a large mixing bowl:

	The boiled & drained POTATOES
3 cups	RICOTTA CHEESE that has been whipped until fluffy
1/2 cup	SOUR CREAM
2 cups	CELERY, chopped
11/2 cups	DRIED CHERRIES or substitute cut up Sundried Tomatoes
1/2 cup	GREEN ONIONS, chopped, or Red Onion
	or use both to equal 1/2 cup
1/2 cup	Fresh BASIL, chopped
1/2 cup	Fresh PARSLEY (flat or curly), chopped
11/2 tbsps.	Dry ROSEMARY or fresh, finely chopped
1-2	GARLIC cloves, minced
2 tbsps.	VINEGAR - white or cider
1	LEMON, juice of
	SALT, PEPPER, & Hot Sauce to taste

Mix together until well combined.
Optional - Stir in:

1 cup	GORGONZOLA or Blue Cheese, crumbled

Transfer to a serving bowl and chill. Toss before serving.

◆◆◆◆◆◆◆◆

Optional: Garnish with sliced red onion, dried cherries and shaved or grated parmesan, romano, fontinella or asiago cheese.

19

ITALIAN POTATO~PARSLEY SALAD

This Italian version takes the humdrum out of usual potato salad.

I can't tell you how many times I have made this salad people always enjoy it, so I just keep making it.

◆◆◆◆◆◆◆◆

Serves 6-8

Boil:

8-10 cups	RED POTATOES, unpeeled, cut into cubes

Cook until tender but not mushy
Drain.

Add to a large mixing bowl:

	Cooked, drained POTATOES
2 cups	PARSLEY, chopped
2 stalks	CELERY, chopped
3/4 cup	CHIVES or Green Onions, chopped
3/4 cup	BLACK OLIVES, sliced
1 medium	RED ONION, sliced
1/3 cup	Extra Virgin OLIVE OIL
1/3 cup	PARMESAN Cheese, grated or shaved
1/3 cup	RED WINE VINEGAR,
1/8 cup	BALSAMIC VINEGAR
1-2	Cloves GARLIC, minced
2 tbsps.	BASIL, fresh, chopped - or 1 teaspoon dry
1 1/2 tsps.	OREGANO, dry
	SALT & PEPPER to taste

Toss until thoroughly mixed.

Taste and adjust seasonings to suit your tastes.
Refrigerate. Serve cold. Toss before serving.

◆◆◆◆◆◆◆◆

Note: This can be made up a few days in advance.
It holds up well and tastes great after marinating a couple days.

GRILLED SUMMER SALAD

(See Photo)

This is one of my all time favorites. Grilling enhances the flavor of the vegetables. Even with no dressing, they're delicious.

Talented photo stylist and girlfriend Shirley Myers assisted in arranging this platter for the photo. It was artfully and skillfully done thanks to her.

◆◆◆◆◆◆◆◆

Serves 6-8

Prepare vegetables for grilling:

2-3	ZUCCHINI, cut off ends & slice lengthwise, into 3 long slices
	(you can use green and yellow or yellow summer squash)
2-3	PEPPERS, Red, Green, Yellow &/or Brown - Hot peppers optional
	cut in half, seeded
2	RED ONIONS, cut into 4 thick slices
1	EGGPLANT, cut off ends & slice horizontally into 4-5 long slices

Optional:

Zucchini Blossoms, leave whole

Portabello Mushroom caps, leave whole

Fennel bulbs, slice lengthwise into 2 or three long slices

Asparagus, leave whole and steam for 2 minutes before grilling

Carrots, use young slender ones, leave whole. Boil until tender before grilling.

Green Beans, steam for 2 minutes. Tie into bundles using the long green part of a green onion. Steam it also, so it becomes flexible and easy to use.

Swiss Chard, leave whole. Dip in water, then put on grill so it sizzles & cooks fast.

Grill vegetables until tender, turning to prevent burning.

Arrange on platter.

Sprinkle with:

2 tsps.	ROSEMARY, leaf, dry or fresh chopped
1 tsp. Each:	BASIL, OREGANO, THYME
	SALT & PEPPER to taste

Drizzle with:

1/4-1/3 cup OLIVE OIL

1/4-1/3 cup VINEGAR

Serve warm, at room temperature or chilled.

◆◆◆◆◆◆◆◆

21

TONY PANOZZO'S
HOMEGROWN SLICED TOMATOES

(See Photo)

I learned this beautiful, simple salad from my dad. As an Agri-Producer of over 2,000 acres, this is a man who really knows produce, from the roots up. It is very important to only use homegrown tomatoes - otherwise, don't bother.

As his mother, my Nona would say "Everything in it's season." All of my family strongly adheres to her philosophy for optimum taste and peak flavor.

Figure 2-3 servings per tomato

Slice ripe homegrown TOMATOES about 1/4" to 1/2 " thick.
Slice as many tomatoes you need.

Arrange overlapping slices on a platter.

Top with a few slices of thinly sliced red onion.

Salt and pepper to taste.

Drizzle with VINEGAR and OLIVE OIL
We just use cider vinegar and regular olive oil, using about equal amounts of each, but it is entirely up to you. Not too much though. It's the fresh taste of the tomatoes that are the most important thing here.

My father notes it is important to put the vinegar and oil on at this point, so it disperses the salt and pepper.

Serve and enjoy!

Option: Top with sliced fresh basil orsliced green pepper rings.
Take one of these thick, juicy slices of dressed tomatoes and put it on a slice of buttered bread. Now that's eating!

CAULIFLOWER SALAD
WITH NON FAT YOGURT DRESSING

Even though this salad has no added fat, it doesn't mean it is lacking flavor.
It is tangy and satisfying.

◆◆◆◆◆◆◆◆

Serves
4 -6

Steam 1 large head CAULIFLOWER,
      3-5 minutes or until barely tender. Do not over cook.
      Drain, divide into flowerets and set aside.

Add to a mixing bowl:
3/4 cup	Non Fat Plain YOGURT
1 tbsp.	LEMON JUICE
1/4 tsp.	Grated LEMON RIND
1/4 tsp.	MACE

Mix well.

Add:
      Steamed CAULIFLOWER
      SALT & PEPPER to taste
Toss until well combined.

Serve at room temperature or chilled. Toss before serving.

◆◆◆◆◆◆◆◆

Sprinkle the top with sesame seeds.
Garnish with lemon slices.

23

SPICED CAULIFLOWER SALAD

Cauliflower actually comes into its own here with the help of a little pickling spice. Who knows, your kids may actually try a taste.

◆◆◆◆◆◆◆◆

Serves 4-8

Fill a large pot, half full of water, add:

    1 tbsp.   PICKLING SPICE, loose or tied up in a piece of cheese cloth. A coffee filter works instead of cheese cloth.

Bring to boil. Let simmer 5-10 minutes. Bring back to boil.

Add:

        A pinch of salt

        A large head of CAULIFLOWER, washed & outer leaves trimmed off. Leave the small, tender inner ones.

Cook covered, until barley tender, 3-5 minutes.
Do not overcook.
Drain.   Remove core and divide into flowers.
Transfer to a mixing bowl.

Add:

    1/2 cup   RED ONION, sliced thin
    2 tbsps.   Red Wine VINEGAR
    1 tbsp.   OLIVE OIL
              SALT & PEPPER to taste

Toss together.
Serve warm, room temperature or chilled. Toss before serving.

◆◆◆◆◆◆◆◆

This makes a great cold side for summer picnics.

SPRING SALAD

This salad has a beautiful blend of colors and textures reminiscent of toubouli. The mint gives it a clean, fresh taste.

◆◆◆◆◆◆◆◆

Serves 4-6

Add to a large mixing bowl:

3/4 cup	CRACKED WHEAT
4	TOMATOES, sliced into wedges
2	CUCUMBERS, unpeeled, sliced
1 small	RED ONION, sliced into thin rings
1 cup	PARSLEY, chopped
1 cup	Fresh MINT, chopped
1/2 cup	LEMON JUICE
1/4 cup	Extra Virgin OLIVE OIL
1 tbsp.	VINEGAR
1 tbsp.	OREGANO
	SALT and PEPPER to taste

Toss well.

Refrigerate for a few hours or overnight.

The cracked wheat softens from the juices of the vegetables. Toss before serving.

If you want to serve the salad immediately, be sure to first soak the cracked wheat in hot water for 10 minutes. Drain it then add it to the salad.

Optional: Top it with crumbled feta cheese and Greek olives.

◆◆◆◆◆◆◆◆

Using olive oil as opposed to extra virgin olive gives this spring salad a lighter, fresher taste.

LOW FAT BROCCOLI - FENNEL SALAD

With the addition of cauliflower and oranges this makes a colorful and nutritious salad.

◆◆◆◆◆◆◆◆

Serves 4-8

Steam the following until barely tender:

1 bunch	BROCCOLI, or Broccolini, (which is a cross between broccoli and Chinese Kale).
1 large	FENNEL BULB {Reserve the stalks and tops}
1 small	Head CAULIFLOWER, cored

{When steaming vegetables, you can add some slices of oranges for flavor. Discard them after vegetables are steamed.}

Drain.

Cut vegetables into large bite size pieces.

Add to a large mixing bowl:

	The cut up VEGETABLES from above
	The reserved FENNEL, stalks and leafy tops
1	ORANGE, grated peel of
2	ORANGES, peeled and sliced
1/2 small	RED ONION, thinly sliced
1/4 cup	Frozen ORANGE JUICE CONCENTRATE, thawed
1 tbsp.	VINEGAR
1 tbsp.	HONEY
2 tsps.	OIL
	SALT and PEPPER to taste

Toss well.

Serve warm, room temperature or chilled. Toss before serving.

*Save any dressing left in the bottom of the bowl.
Use it drizzled over salad greens.*

◆◆◆◆◆◆◆◆

This salad is attractive garnished with red flower blossoms or topped with seasonal fresh fruits.

CABBAGE - BERRY SALAD

This is a light summer salad. The berries are an unexpected and pleasant surprise.

◆◆◆◆◆◆◆◆

*Serves
4-8*

Add to a large mixing bowl:

1 head	CABBAGE, shredded
1/2	RED ONION, sliced thinly
1	Red or Green PEPPER, sliced thinly
1/2 cup	VINEGAR
1/4 cup	HONEY
1/4 cup	SUGAR
3-4 tbsps.	OIL
	SALT and PEPPER to taste

Toss well.
Chill until ready to serve.

Before serving, add:

    2 cups   BERRIES - use any or a combination of:
Blueberries, Red Raspberries, Black Raspberries,
Blackberries and/or sliced Strawberries.

Toss and serve.

Garnish with additional berries.

◆◆◆◆◆◆◆◆

*Making this up a day in advance lowers some of the crispy factor of the cabbage.
Some like it crisp, some like it not. You decide.*

JIM RANKIN'S CRANBERRY MOLD

If you are looking for a traditional mold with a nontraditional flavor, this is it. Sour cream and a dash of horseradish give it a really unique flavor.

Serves 4-6

Make Cranberry Sauce.

CRANBERRY SAUCE

Add to a medium saucepan:

2 cups	SUGAR
1 1/2 cups	WATER
Pinch of	SALT

Bring to boil and cook 5-10 minutes.

Add:

4 cups	CRANBERRIES
Zest of 1	ORANGE

Stir and simmer 10-15 minutes more. Remove zest.

CRANBERRY MOLD

In a medium saucepan, soften:

1 pk.	UNFLAVORED GELATIN	in	1/2 cup	COLD WATER

Let set for 5-10 minutes to soften.
Heat and stir until gelatin is dissolved. Remove from heat.

Add stirring:

2 cups	CRANBERRY SAUCE
1 cup	SOUR CREAM
4 tbsps.	HORSERADISH
Juice of 1	LEMON
Pinch of	SALT

Pour into oiled ring mold and refrigerate until firm and remove from mold.
The easiest way to unmold is to use a plastic mold with a removable top and bottom. This releases the vacuum pressure and the gelatine drops out.
Place romaine leaves on a platter and unmold.
Garnish with orange and lemon slices.

FALL HARVEST SALAD

This is a wonderful fall salad that is made with apples, sweet potatoes and cabbage. It is enhanced with molasses, maple syrup raisins and a bit of pie spice.

◆◆◆◆◆◆◆◆

Serves 4-8

Add to a large mixing bowl:

1 head	CABBAGE, shredded (use a small head or 1/2 of a large head)	
4	APPLES, unpeeled, sliced	
2 small	SWEET POTATOES, raw, peeled and grated, shredded or julienned	
1 cup	RAISINS or chopped Dates	
1/3 cup	MAPLE SYRUP or Pancake Syrup	
1/4 cup	VINEGAR - preferably, Cider Vinegar	
1/4 cup	CORN OIL, Vegetable or Canola	
3 tbsps.	MOLASSES or Sorghum	
2 tsps.	PIE SPICE	
	SALT and PEPPER to taste	

Toss well.

Chill until ready to serve. Toss before serving.

Garnish with walnuts or pecans.

For a fall buffet, serve this salad in a pumpkin shell and surround it with fall leaves.

JICIMA SALAD
WITH COCONUT MILK & ADZUKI BEANS

This is for my Mexico going girlfriends Martha Mosier Reynolds and Sharon Pierce, both who demonstrate a passion for the arts, fine food and a spiritual life.

◆◆◆◆◆◆◆◆

Serves 4-6

Add to a large mixing bowl:

5 cups	JICIAMA, peeled and grated
3 cups	SWISS CHARD, sliced, steamed and drained; or frozen, thawed, chopped and drained
2 cups	ADZUKI BEANS, cooked and drained or canned and drained
1/2 cup	COCONUT MILK
1/4 cup	SUGAR
1/4 cup	VINEGAR
3-4 tbsps.	CORN OIL or Olive Oil
	SALT and PEPPER to taste

Toss well.
Refrigerate until ready to serve.
Toss before serving.

◆◆◆◆◆◆◆◆

Serve on fresh Swiss Chard leaves or use coconut halves as salad bowls. Top with shaved coconut.
Don't underestimate this salad. It is perfect when you are looking for something unique to serve.

ASPARAGUS VINAIGRETTE

For spring and summer, this is sooooo easy!
No measuring. Just do it!

◆◆◆◆◆◆◆◆

Wash and stem
one or two bunches of ASPARAGUS.
Steam to al dente.

Arrange on a platter.

Garnish
with RED ONION slices
chopped hard boiled EGG or Egg Whites
and ORANGE ZESTS

Make zests from the orange, holding the orange over the platter, letting the oils
spray the asparagus, giving it a scent of citrus.

Sprinkle
with SALT and PEPPER.

Drizzle
with VINEGAR and OLIVE OIL. (Not extra virgin olive oil.)

◆◆◆◆◆◆◆◆

Serve warm, room temperature or chilled.

This is one dish I traditionally served at Panozzo's Cafe for Easter Brunch.
A wonderful way to say spring is on the way!

31

CARROT APPLE SALAD

This salad is a real kid pleaser because it has peanut butter in the dressing.
They will never know they are eating carrots.

◆◆◆◆◆◆◆◆

Serves 6-8

Add to a bowl:

4	APPLES, cut up into bite size pieces - not peeled
2 cups	Grated CARROTS
2 cups	Chopped CELERY
1/2 cup	RAISINS or dried Cranberries
1 cup	WALNUTS or PEANUTS optional

Set aside.

Make "Peanut - Orange Dressing"

PEANUT ORANGE DRESSING

Add to a blender:

1/2 cup	ORANGE JUICE
3-4 tbsp.	PEANUT BUTTER (heaping)

Blend until smooth and creamy.

If you want a thicker dressing, add more peanut butter. This consistency makes a great vegetable or fruit dip. For a thinner dressing add more orange juice This makes a nice salad dressing.

Pour desired amount of dressing over apple-carrot mixture, just before serving.
{If the mixture is tossed together too far in advance, the apples juice up and the salad becomes watery.}
Toss until well combined.

◆◆◆◆◆◆◆◆

For a terrific pita pocket stuffer, look no further. Tuck in a little bit of lettuce for added texture. This one really hits the spot!

ROMAINE & ESCAROLE SALAD WITH HEARTS OF PALM

This is one of those salads that is hard to quit eating. For salad lovers, like my girlfriend Kathleen Kennedy-Shepherd, you need not serve any other course!

◆◆◆◆◆◆◆◆

Fill a large salad bowl 3/4 full of:
ROMAINE, washed, drained well and torn up
ESCAROLE, washed, drained well and torn up
{Or you can use any combination of gourmet greens.}

Add:

6-8	HEARTS OF PALM - canned or frozen, drained	
	(Pull apart palm as you would rope cheese)	
6-8	ARTICHOKE HEARTS - canned, drained	
	(Cut into halves or quarters)	
1	RED PEPPER, grilled and sliced	
	(Or slice it & saute it in a little olive oil)	
1/2	RED ONION, sliced into thin rings	
1 cup	LENTILS - cooked or canned, drained	
	(Options: omit or you can use any kind of legume.)	
1/2 cup	ASIAGO CHEESE, shaved	
1/3 cup	PARMESAN or Romano cheese, grated	
1 tsp. each:	OREGANO and MARJORAM, dry	
1/3 cup	OLIVE OIL	
2 tbsps.	Extra Virgin OLIVE OIL	
1/3 cup	VINEGAR	
2 tbsps.	BALSAMIC VINEGAR	
1	AVOCADO - ripe, sliced	
	SALT and PEPPER to taste	

Toss well and serve.

◆◆◆◆◆◆◆◆

A crusty French or Italian bread is a 'must' with this salad.

SAUTÉD CHICKEN ATOP
GOURMET GREENS

*Definitely a meal at lunch or dinner time. Salad connoisseurs give this one
a very high rating.*

◆◆◆◆◆◆◆◆

Serves 2 generously as a Main Course

Add to a large sauté pan, over medium heat:

1/8-1/4 cup	Extra Virgin OLIVE OIL
2	CHICKEN BREASTS, skinless, boneless, sliced
1 cup	MUSHROOMS, sliced
1/2 cup	LEEKS, cut up and wash very well. They are usually sandy.
1 small	RED ONION, thinly sliced
1-2 cloves	GARLIC, minced
1/4 cup	BALSAMIC VINEGAR
1/8 cup	VERMOUTH
1/2 tsp.	THYME, dry
1/2 tsp.	OREGANO, dry
1/4 tsp.	ROSEMARY, dry or 1/2 tsp. fresh, chopped
	SALT & PEPPER to taste

Cook covered until chicken is done, about 15-25 minutes.
Stir occasionally, while cooking.

While this is cooking, place mounds of GOURMET GREENS on 2 dinner plates. (Or 3-4
plates for smaller potions.)
Serve warm, dividing mixture evenly over plates of greens.

Top with PARMESAN CHEESE, crumbled FETA CHEESE and chopped TOMATO.

◆◆◆◆◆◆◆◆

*This works great as a grilled salad.
Grill the chicken breasts and mushrooms whole. Slice the leeks in half lengthwise for
grilling. Cut them up and toss with the rest of the ingredients.*

SWEETHEART OF A SALAD

(See Photo)

Keep it easy & Fun.
Try to get out of the habit of measuring. Just start throwing in ingredients.
Then, season to your own tastes. Add your own flair!

◆◆◆◆◆◆◆◆

Serves 2-6

Add to a large sauté pan, over medium heat:

1/4 cup	TOASTED PUMPKIN GRAPESEED OIL*
1/4 cup	SPICY PECAN VINEGAR*
1 large	SWEET POTATO - raw, peeled & julienned (cut like french fries)or cut into small cubes
1 medium	RED ONION, thinly sliced
1 tsp.	THYME, dried or fresh
1/2 cup	Dried CRANBERRIES, CHERRIES or chopped dates
1 tblsp.	BROWN SUGAR
	SALT & PEPPER to taste

NOTE: If you want to cut down on the fat content, decrease the oil and substitute it for the same amount of orange juice.

Cook covered until sweet potatoes are tender, stirring occassionally.
While this is cooking, place mounds of GOURMET GREENS on 2 dinner plates. (Or 3-4 plates for smaller potions.)

Serve warm, dividing mixture evenly over plates of greens.

Sprinkle top with: Shelled, roasted pumpkin seed or roasted pecans.
Garnish with orange wedges.

◆◆◆◆◆◆◆◆

For Valentine's Day,
garnish with beet slices cut in the shape of hearts.
(You can use an aspic cutter to do this.)

*These items are available at gourmet food shops.

35

TUNA PINEAPPLE SALAD

For all the years I had Panozzo's Cafe, this sandwich stuffer always stayed on the menu. Pineapple, raisins and grated carrots give it a slight sweetness that is satisfying and delicious.

◆◆◆◆◆◆◆◆

Serves 6-10

Add to a mixing bowl:

1 6 oz. can	TUNA - in spring water, well drained
1-14 oz. can	PINEAPPLE TIDBITS, well drained
1 cup	Chopped CELERY
1/2 cup	Grated CARROTS
1/2 cup	RAISINS (they will soften in the salad)
1/2 cup	SOUR CREAM
1/2 cup	MIRACLE WHIP or MAYONNAISE, "light" or regular

Mix untill well combined. Refrigerate.
When serving it the next day, you may want to pour off any juices that have accumulated.

FRESH TUNA PINEAPPLE SALAD

This is the updated version of the old favorite.

◆◆◆◆◆◆◆◆

Serves 6-10

Add to a mixing bowl:

6-8 ozs.	TUNA STEAK, grilled and cut up
2 cups	Fresh PINEAPPLE, peeled, cored and cut up into tidbits
1 cup	Seedless RED GRAPES
1 cup	Fresh FENNEL, chopped
1/2 cup	CARROTS, julienned, madolined into long threads, or grated
1/2 cup	GOAT CHEESE, softened
1/4 cup	GRAPESEED OIL
1/4 cup	LEMON JUICE

Mix until well combined. Refrigerate.

◆◆◆◆◆◆◆◆

Serve these in sandwiches with lettuce and tomato. Great in pita bread, on toasted english muffins, stuffed into tomato shells or atop salad greens.

GRANDMA RASPOLICH'S
DANDELIONS & POTATOES

*My Croatian Grandma, Ida, would pick dandelions early in the spring,
when their leaves are tender and long before they sprout blooms.
Domestic varieties are now grown and can usually be found in
supermarkets with great produce sections. Or look for the seeds and plant
them in your garden. No more is it a peasant food.
It is now in the list of gourmet greens.*

Serves 4-6

Clean, wash, drain and set aside:
>1 lb. (approx.)   DANDELION GREENS or substitute fresh spinach

Thinly slice and set aside:
>1 small   RED ONION

Boil in salted water:
>1-1 1/2 lbs.   New RED POTATOES, cut into large chunks

Cook until potatoes are very tender and nearly mushy.
Drain.
Transfer to large wooden salad bowl.

Add:
>1-2 cloves   GARLIC, sliced or minced

Mash the garlic with the potatoes. Do not over mash. The potatoes should be kind of chunky.

While the potatoes are still hot, add the:
>DANDELION GREENS
>RED ONION, thinly sliced
>SALT & PEPPER to taste

Drizzle with:
>1/3 cup   EXTRA VIRGIN OLIVE OIL
>1/4 cup   CIDER VINEGAR

Toss together.
Serve warm or at room temperature.
Note: The potatoes must still be hot so the greens wilt down a bit.

*Wild dandelions are a delicacy to my family.
My relatives would walk the roadsides and pastures picking them. My grandpa Raspolich
even invented a tool to cut them at the base while standing, eliminating all the bending.
You can tell we are serious dandelion lovers.*

For therapeutic reasons,
do a little baking.

There is something very
soothing about the aromas
that fill the room.

Then there is the sharing.

See, how good it feels.

BREADS

Honey-Fig Muffins

*Not just any breakfast muffins. These will dress up a brunch or add a
special touch to a luncheon.*

Makes about 2 dozen regular or 12 large

Preheat oven to 375⁰ F.

Add to a mixing bowl:

4 cups	White FLOUR
1 tbsp.	BAKING POWDER
1 cup	SUGAR
1/2 tsp.	each: CARDOMOM, ALLSPICE, & MACE

Mix well.

Add:

2	EGGS, beaten
11/2 cup	PRUNE JUICE, Apricot or Orange Juice or mixture of
1/3 cup	HONEY
1/2 cup	CORN OIL, Vegetable Oil or melted Butter
1 tsp.	Grated ORANGE PEEL
1 cup	Ripe, fresh FIGS, stems cut off & chopped, or DRIED FIGS, softened in hot water, drained and chopped

Stir until well blended, but do not over mix since this will cause them
to be rubbery.
If you overmix, let batter rest for at least 15 minutes. This relaxes the elasticity.

The batter should be thick but not too thick, nor too thin. The moisture content
of the figs has a direct bearing on the consistency of the batter. If the batter is
too stiff, add more juice. If the batter is too thin, add more flour.

Fill paper-lined muffin [cupcake] pans to the top or oil nonstick pans.
Using an ice-cream scoop to do this works well.

Sprinkle tops with ROLLED OATS or NUTS.

Bake at 375°F for 20-30 minutes, or until lightly browned and firm to the touch.

*To give these muffins a taste of the yultide season, add various chopped
dried fruits and nuts.*

Low Fat Multigrain Muffins
Strawberry-Lemon-Kiwi

These are perfect for spring and summer. They also do nicely for Easter and Mothers' Day. When the Fourth of July rolls around, substitute kiwi for blueberries and have RED, WHITE & BLUE MUFFINS.

Makes about 2 dozen regular or 12 large

Preheat oven to 375° F.

To a mixing bowl add:

3 1/2 cups	WHITE FLOUR
1/2 cup	WHOLE WHEAT FLOUR
1 cup	ROLLED OATS
1/2 cup	CORNMEAL
2 cups	SUGAR
1 tbsp.	BAKING POWDER

Mix together.

Add:

4	EGG WHITES, beaten or 1/3 cup egg substitute
1 cup	STRAWBERRIES, cleaned and cut up into small pieces
1 cup	KIWI, peeled and cut up into small pieces
1 cup	ORANGE JUICE
1 cup	SKIM MILK
1/2 cup	LEMON JUICE
1 tbsp.	VINEGAR
1/4 tsp.	SALT
2-4	Dashes of BITTERS
	Grated peel of 1 LEMON

Mix until well blended, but do not overmix since this will cause them to be rubbery.

If you overmix, let batter rest for at least 15 minutes. This relaxes the elasticity.

The batter should be thick but not too thick, nor too thin. The fruits being dry or moist, has a direct bearing on the consistency of the batter. So, make the necessary adjustments. If the batter is too stiff add more O.J. or skim milk. If is too thin add more white flour.

Fill paper-lined muffin [cupcake] pans to the top or oil nonstick pans.
Using an ice-cream scoop to do this works well.
Coat the tops with:

LEMON-SUGAR TOPPING:

Mix together 1 cup SUGAR with grated peel of 1 LEMON

Bake at 375°F for 20-30 minutes, until lightly browned and firm to the touch.

41

Country Morning Muffins

*Choose your favorite fruit to put in these yummy,
easy to bake muffins.*

Let's use the "one bowl-less mess" method to keep this really easy!

Makes about 2 dozen regular or 12 large

Preheat oven to 375⁰ F.

Add to a large mixing bowl:

3 cups	WHITE FLOUR
1/2 cup	BRAN or Bran Cereal
1/2 cup	ROLLED OATS
1 cup	SUGAR (or 1/2 cup of Honey)
1 tbsp.	BAKING SODA
1 tsp.	CINNAMON or Pie Spice

Mix together.

Add:

2	EGGS, beaten, or 1/3 cup egg substitute for lower fat
2 cups	ORANGE JUICE or fruit juice of your choice
1/4 cup	CORN OIL or Vegetable Oil
1 tsp.	ALMOND EXTRACT or Vanilla Extract
1 cup	FRESH FRUIT - cut up (or dried fruits and/or chopped nuts) [Berries, such as blueberries and raspberries, leave whole.]

Mix until well combined. Over mixing makes them rubbery.
If you overmix, let batter rest for at least 15 minutes. This relaxes the elastiity.

The batter should not be thick but not too thick, nor too thin. The fruits being dry or moist, has a direct bearing on the consistency of the batter. So, make the necessary adjustments. If the batter is too, stiff add more O.J. If is too thin, add more white flour.

Fill paper-lined muffin [cupcake] pans to the top or oil nonstick pans.
Using an ice-cream scoop to do this works well.

OPTION: Sprinkle the tops with granola, rolled oats, cinnamon &/or sugar.

Bake at 375°F for 20-30 minutes, until lightly browned and firm to the touch.

Chestnut &
Dried Cherry Scones

A hint of cardamom make these drop scones perfect for the Yuletide Season. Serve these with lemon or raspberry curd, available at gourmet stores and Panozzo's Pantry in Chesterton, Indiana.

Makes 9-12

Preheat oven to 375⁰ F.

Add to a large mixing bowl:

2 cups	White FLOUR
1 cup	SUGAR
2/3 cup	CHESTNUT MEATS, cooked and chopped
2/3 cup	DRIED CHERRIES that have been softened in hot water. Drained.
1 tbsp.	Grated ORANGE RIND
2 tsps.	BAKING POWDER
1 tsp.	CARDAMOM
1/4 tsp. each	ALLSPICE, NUTMEG, CINNAMON
1/4 tsp.	SALT
1	Large EGG, beaten
3/4 cup	ORANGE JUICE
8 tbsps.	BUTTER (I stick), softened

Stir together until a sticky dough forms.
If necessary, add a little more flour to firm it up.

Drop 1/4 cupfuls of dough, 2" apart on ungreased cookie sheet.

Sprinkle the tops with desired amounts of sugar and cinnamon.
Bake in preheated oven at 375°F for 20-25 minutes, until lightly browned.

Serve warm or cool on wire racks before storing.

Besides a breakfast treat, these go nicely accompanying a salad topped with duck or smoked turkey.

Red Pepper Jelly Biscuits

Instead of muffins, danish, or doughnuts, try these mouth watering biscuits that have a wonderful "kick".

Preheat oven to 375^0 F.

To make this really easy:
    Use a biscuit mix, follow package directions.   Make desired amount.

Roll dough to 1/2 " thickness.
Cut in squares or circles about 2" wide

Or use refrigerated biscuits and separate.

Sugar-Cinnamon Topping

Mix together:
2/3 cup	SUGAR
2 tsps.	CINNAMON
1/2 tsp.	ALLSPICE

Set aside.

Dip each biscuit in melted BUTTER, then in sugar-cinnamon mix.

Place on ungreased cookie sheet.

Make a deep thumb print in the center of each biscuit.

Fill with RED PEPPER JELLY, available in supermarkets.

Bake at 375^0 F for 15-20 minutes, or until edges are golden brown.

The sweet and tangy combination make for a versatile biscuit for breakfast, lunch or dinner.

Fresh Blueberry Coffee Cake

This is an old time favorite done in a quick, one-bowl method that will give you excellent results.

Serves 6-8

Preheat oven to 375⁰ F.

Add to a large mixing bowl:

3/4 cup	BUTTER or Margarine (1 1/2 sticks), softened	
1 1/2 cup	SUGAR	
1 cup	SOUR CREAM	
4	EGGS	
1 tsp.	VANILLA	

Mix until thoroughly blended.

Add:

3 cups	FLOUR
1 1/2 tsp.	BAKING POWDER
1/2 tsp.	BAKING SODA
1/2 tsp.	CINNAMON
1/4 tsp.	SALT

Mix until thoroughly blended.

Add:

2 cups	BLUEBERRIES, fresh

Fold carefully into batter, trying not to crush berries.

Pour into oiled 13"x 9" baking dish.

Sprinkle with SUGAR - SPICE TOPPING:
Mix together 1/3 cup SUGAR with 1 teaspoon PIE SPICE

Bake at 375⁰ F for 30-40 minutes or until golden brown.

This is delicious served warm, right out of the oven!

Onion-Beer Skillet Bread

*This is delicious served warm. It goes great with soups, stews, and salads.
Add it to your Super Bowl menu! Try using a craft beer from a Micro
Brewery to add to its flavor.*

Makes two 8" or 9" skillets

Add to a large bowl:

2 cups	BEER - measure liquid level, excluding foam level. Heated to 105° - 115° F.
1 pkg.	quick rise YEAST

Mix until yeast is dissolved.

Add:

4 cups	BAKING MIX (Jiffy, Bisquik, Arrow Head Mill, etc.)
4 cups	BREAD FLOUR (high gluten)
1/4 cup	SUGAR
1/2 tsp.	SALT or - more or less to your liking
4	Large EGGS, beaten

Stir until well mixed. Continue mixing for a few minutes.

Cover and let rest 10 minutes.
Stir again for a few minutes and divide between 2 oiled 8" or 9" cast iron skillet
with no flammable handles. Or use baking dishes.
To even out the dough in the pans use lightly floured fingers.
Make topping.

Onion Topping

Add to a small skillet over medium heat:

1 tbsp.	BUTTER
1/2 cup	ONION, chopped
3 tbsps.	BEER

Sauté until onions are transparent.

Spoon over dough.
Cover with plastic wrap and let rise for 30 - 45 minutes in warm place.
Preheat oven to 375⁰ F.
Bake at 375° F. oven for about 25 - 35 minutes, or until edges are golden brown.

Cherry Espresso Bread

A yeast bread that has dried cherries and hint of espresso. It is perfect for dunking. My Grandfather, Joe Raspolich, used to make a breakfast out of dunking slice after slice of crusty bread into a steaming bowl of hot coffee. He lived to be 100. I make this bread with him in mind, thinking of how much he would have enjoyed it.

Makes 2 loaves

Add to large mixing bowl:

2 cups	ESPRESSO or use strong coffee, brewed, 105° - 115° F. If necessary add 1 - teaspoons instant coffee to make it strong.
1 pkg.	Quick Rise YEAST

Mix until yeast is dissolved.
Add:

1 1/2 cups	DRIED CHERRIES

Allow to sit for 5-10 minutes so cherries can soften.
Add:

2 tbsps.	SUGAR
2 tbsps.	RASPBERRY VINEGAR or any fruit vinegar
3/4 tsp.	SALT
1	EGG, beaten
5-6 cups	BREAD FLOUR (high gluten)

Note: Stir in enough flour to make a moderate stiff dough, then add more as you knead. Mix until well combined. Knead by hand on floured work surface or with a mixer fitted with a dough hook.

Knead until smooth, shiny and elastic. Cover and let rest 10 minutes.
Knead again for about 5 minutes.
Shape into two loaves. Place on oiled baking sheets.

Mix together:

1/4 cup	WATER
1 tsp.	CORNSTARCH

Brush tops with some of this mixture.
Sprinkle tops heavily with SUGAR. Slash diagonal cuts on top. Let rise until double in size.
Preheat oven to 375° F.

Bake in a 375°F oven, for about 25 - 35 minutes or until golden brown.

47

Spicy Herb-Onion Bread

This most delicious bread is sure to be a favorite of any self-appointed bread connoisseur.

Makes 2 large loaves or several smaller loaves

Add to a large mixing bowl:

2 1/2 cups	Warm WATER, 105°-115° F.
2 pkg.	Quick Rise YEAST

Mix until yeast is dissolved.

Add:

1 tsp.	SALT
1 tsp.	SUGAR
1 tsp.	Ground MUSTARD
1 tsp.	BASIL
1 tsp.	BLACK PEPPER - coarsely ground
2 tsp.	Leaf ROSEMARY - crumbled
1 tbsp.	OLIVE OIL
1 tbsp.	Dried crushed hot RED PEPPER
1 clove	GARLIC - minced
1 cup	Chopped, cooked ONIONS
6-7 cups	BREAD FLOUR [high gluten]

Mix until well combined.

Note: Stir in enough flour to make a moderate stiff dough, then add more as you knead. Work in more flour to make a sturdy, smooth, elastic dough.

Knead by hand on floured work surface or with a mixer fitted with a dough hook. Knead until smooth, shiny and elastic. Place dough in a lightly oiled large bowl. The bowl should be twice the size of the dough to allow for rising. Invert the dough so the oiled side is up, to prevent the dough from drying out. Cover and put in a warm place until double in bulk, about 1/2 hr.

After rising, knead dough on a floured surface for about 5 minutes.
Shape into desired loaves. Place on oiled baking sheets dusted with cornmeal. Dust tops with flour. Slash diagonal cuts on top with a sharp knife. Let rise for 1/2 hour or until double in size.

Preheat oven to 400° F.

Bake in 400° F.
Bake until loaves are golden brown, 20-40 minutes, depending on size of loaves.

Eggplant Filled Bread

This bread is filled with an Italian-style eggplant filling. Whether it's 'pasta time' or' picnic time', this bread is perfect.

1. Make "**ROASTED ITALIAN EGGPLANT FILLING**". See recipe below.
2. Make half the recipe of the "**SPICY HERB ONION BREAD**' from the preceding page (p48). Cover and let rise in warm place until double in size.
3. Divide dough in half.
4. Press half of the dough into a the bottom of a lightly oiled 8" spring form pan. Press the dough one inch or more, up the sides of the pan.
5. Moisten edges of dough with water.
6. Place filling on dough.
7. Roll out rest of dough in a circle large enough to fit on top of the filling, being sure that it reaches the inside edge of the pan.
8. Place 2nd piece of dough on top of filling. Make sure that the bottom and top doughs are touching. Press and pinch the doughs together to seal.
9. Dust the top with flour. Make 2-3 slashes on the top with a knife.
10. Let rise 20 -30 minutes.

    Preheat oven to 375⁰ F.
11. Bake 400°F for 30-40 minutes until lightly browned.
12. Remove from spring form pan. Serve warm.

Roasted Italian Eggplant Filling

Add to a roasting pan:

2-4 tblsps.	OLIVE OIL, Extra Virgin
1 small	EGGPLANT, not peeled, cut up into small cubes
1	ONION, chopped
1-2 cloves	GARLIC, minced

Sprinkle with desired amounts of:

SALT, PEPPER, a little OREGANO, ROSEMARY and PARMESAN CHEESE

Toss well.

Bake in 400° F. oven for 30-45 minutes or until veggies are tender.

Cheese & Bacon Bit Dog Biscuits

This is for all our canine friends that give us love unconditionally. Danny Coval inspired me to add this recipe because of his care and devotion to these wonderful animals.

To a mixing bowl, add;

11/2 cups	WHOLE WHEAT FLOUR (or 1 cup flour & 1/2 cup wheat germ)
11/2 cups	CHEDDAR CHEESE, grated - at room temperature
1/4 -1/2 cup	BACON BITS
1/4 cup	OIL
1 clove	GARLIC, minced
	SALT
	MILK, beef broth or chicken broth

Stir together.
Add enough liquid to form a ball. Chill for 30 minutes.

Roll out on floured surface to about 1/2" thick.
Cut out into desired shapes or use a dog bone shaped cookie cutter. Place 1" apart on lightly oiled cookie sheet. Bake at 350° F. until firm and lightly toasted, 15-30 minutes, depending on the size. (Note: to make them harder, leave them in the oven with the heat turned off for about 1 hour.) Store in air tight container.

Tuna Cat Biscuits

Let's not forget our precious kittens: "Pumpkin" is the queen of the Panozzo kingdom, "Sam" is the Mayor of Furnesville near Panozzo's Pantry and Felix & Oscar are kitty connoisseurs.

To a bowl, add:

2 6 oz. cans	TUNA, drained
2 cups	CORNMEAL
2 cups	FLOUR
2/3 cup	OIL
	WATER, chicken stock or beef stock

Stir together.
Add enough liquid to form a ball, about 1-11/2 cups.

Roll out on floured surface to about 1/2" thick.
Cut out into desired shapes. For cats, cut into small squares. Place 1/2-1" apart on lightly oiled cookie sheet. Bake at 350° F. until firm and lightly toasted, 12-30 minutes, depending on the size. (Note: to make them crunchier, leave them in the oven with the heat turned off for about an hour.) Store in air tight container.

Bowls and bowls

of shear bliss.

The kind of goodness
that warms you all over.

PORTABELLO MUSHROOM AND GOAT CHEESE BISQUE

This is such a delicious combination, I also wrote it as a sauce for pasta, rice, omelets or meats. (See p. 66) Once you start eating it, it's hard to stop! Serve it with a lot of bread to soak up every drop.

Serves 4-8

Add to a 10-12 quart stock pot, over medium heat:

4-6 tbsp.	BUTTER
1 cup	CELERY, chopped
1 cup	LEEKS, chopped
1/2 cup	ONIONS, chopped
1-2 cloves	GARLIC, minced
4-5 cups	PORTABELLO MUSHROOMS, cut up

Sauté until vegetables are tender.
Add:

4 cups	CHICKEN STOCK
2 cups	BEEF STOCK
1/2 cup	DRY VERMOUTH
1 tsp.	CHICKEN BOUILLON
1 tsp.	ROSEMARY, dry or 2 tsps. fresh, chopped
1/2 tsp.	THYME. dry or 1 tsp. fresh, chopped
	SALT & PEPPER to taste

Cook for about 30 minutes until mushrooms are tender and flavors have mixed.
Optional: Add 1-2 cups cooked brown & wild rice for more texture. Heat.

Prepare the goat cheese while soup is cooking.
Add to a microwaveable bowl:

1 cup	GOAT CHEESE (8 oz.)

Pierce holes in cheese. Cover with paper towel or wax paper.
Microwave until cheese is softened. Stir until smooth adding a little of hot broth from the soup to make it easier to stir.
Add GOAT CHEESE to soup, stirring as adding. Adjust seasonings.
Keep on low heat until ready to serve.
Be sure not to bring soup to a boil since this will cause the cheese to curdle.
If making this ahead, reheat over low heat of stove or reheat in microwave to prevent scorching. Stir frequently.

ROASTED RED PEPPER SOUP

*The flavor of the Southwest comes home
with this full bodied soup.*

Serves 6-10

ROASTING THE PEPPERS:

6   DRY ANCHO CHILI PEPPERS

Remove the seeds and veins from the chili peppers. Chop coarsely.
Place in a heavy frying pan over high heat. Toss until lightly toasted.
You should be able to smell the aromas. Add enough water to cover.
Bring to boil, then simmer for about 5 minutes.
Turn off heat and let rest for 5 more minutes. Transfer to a food processor.
Add more water as necessary to make a smooth puree.

MAKING THE SOUP:

Add to a 10-12 quart stock pot, over medium heat:

4 tbsp.	OLIVE OIL
2 medium	ONIONS, chopped
6	RED PEPPERS, chopped
4	Cloves GARLIC, minced

Saute until vegetables are tender.
Add:

6 cups	CHICKEN BROTH
2 cups	POTATO, cut up, unpeeled
1/8 cup	CILANTRO, chopped
	ROASTED PEPPER PUREE from above procedure
1/8 cup	LIME JUICE
1/8 cup	TEQUILA
1/2 tsp.	CUMIN
	SALT, PEPPER & HOT SAUCE to taste

Bring to a boil. Lower heat and simmer for 30-45 minutes.
Make any additions to suit your tastes. More Cilantro, garlic, or tequila?
Serve hot, topped with avocado slices, sour cream and fried tortilla strips.
*Instead of fried tortilla strips, you can use tortilla chips
and just serve them on the side.*

53

CHERYL'S SQUASH SOUP

My dear girlfriend, Cheryl Sloane adapted this from a recipe given to her mother, Joyce Sloane, by one of the women at Second City Comedy Club, in Chicago. Feel free to do variation of this creamy, fall soup adding carrots or pumpkin.

To a stock pot, over medium heat, melt:

    6 tbsps.   BUTTER

Add:

    8-12   SHALLOTS, peeled and diced

    2-3   Granny Smith APPLES, peeled and diced

Sauté until shallots and apples are translucent.

Add:

    1/4 cup   BROWN SUGAR

Continue to sauté until brown sugar caramelizes.

Add, carefully:

    16-20 oz.   VEGETABLE STOCK

Increase heat and bring to boil.

Add:

    2 medium   BUTTERNUT SQUASH, peeled and cut up

    2 medium   SWEET POTATOES, peeled and cut up

Bring back to boil. Reduce heat. Cover, leaving lid ajar. Cook until squash and potatoes are tender, 20-30 minutes. Stir occasionally.

Using a hand held blender, puree to your desired consistency.

Add, while stirring:

    2 cups   MILK or 2% Milk

    1/2 cup   (additional) BROWN SUGAR

    1 tbsp.   CURRY POWDER

              NUTMEG to taste

              SALT & WHITE PEPPER to taste

  optional: 1 or 2 shots of BRANDY or COGNAC

Heat gently while stirring. Do not boil or milk will scorch.

Adjust seasoning. If you like a thinner soup, add more milk or vegetable stock.

Note: This soup is best made a day in advance. Reheat at a low temperature, stirring frequently to prevent scorching.

Top with toasted pecans.

You can flavor the pecans with cayenne, curry powder or brown sugar before toasting. Also tasty with a dollop of sour cream or plain yogurt.

POTATO - LEEK BISQUE

(See Photo)

It's delicious. Hearty yet not too rich. This can be served hot or cold.

Serves 6-10

Add to a 10-12 quart stock pot, over medium heat:

1/4 cup	BUTTER or Oil
1 cup	CELERY, chopped
1 medium	ONION, chopped
1 1/2 cups	LEEKS, thinly sliced - use white and green part
1/2 cup	PARSLEY, chopped
2-3 cloves	GARLIC, minced

Sauté until veggies are tender.

Add:

6 cups	CHICKEN STOCK, fresh or canned
3 cups	POTATO, cubed - red or white, unpeeled
1/2 cup	DRY VERMOUTH
2 tsp.	CHICKEN BOUILLON or 1 teaspoon Chicken Base
1 tsp.	THYME
1 tsp.	SAGE
	SALT, PEPPER & HOT SAUCE to taste

Cook for about 30 minutes until potatoes are tender.
Puree all or part of the soup.   (However it appeals to you.)

Add to a small bowl:

8 oz.	GOAT CHEESE or CREAM CHEESE, softened
	Some of pureed mixture

Stir together until smooth.

Add cheese mixture to soup.
At this point, keep on low heat until ready to serve. Do not bring to a boil since this will cause the cheese to curdle. If making ahead, reheat over low heat on stove,or reheat in microwave to prevent scorching.

Garnish with crumbled Goat Cheese, or a dollop of sour cream.
Plain yogurt can be used also.

MARY ANN'S
MOVE OVER CHICKEN SOUP!

When anyone had a cold or the flu, Mary Ann DeBoo was there with her quick and tasty chicken soup. This soup gives loving comfort along with a pungent flavor that will have them sitting up to taking notice.

Serves however many you need to comfort, or just you!

This soup is a quick and delicious.
The idea is to not be encumbered by a recipe. So study the following, then go to the kitchen and whip it up according to your own liking.

Here are the basics:
Bring CHICKEN BROTH to a boil, fresh or canned.

Add desired amount of the following:

> GARLIC, minced
>
> Fresh GINGER, peeled and minced
>
> GREEN ONIONS, chopped
>
> Fresh CILANTRO, chopped
>
> RED PEPPER FLAKES or Hot Pepper Sauce
>
> LEMON GRASS, white part chopped or juice from 1 LEMON
>
> SALT and PEPPER

It's DONE!
You can bring it back to a boil, but it isn't even necessary.
If you want to take it a step further, here are suggestions for additional ingredients:

> SHRIMP , or any kind of fish or seafood
>
> MUSHROOMS, there's a wide variety
>
> EGG, raw & beaten, for an egg drop soup,
>
> RICE, cooked
>
> NOODLES, cooked
>
> VEGGIES, cut up
>
> SOY SAUCE
>
> FISH SAUCE.

Debby (Tomecek) Pleva knows the care that came from our big hearted friend, Mary Ann. So, make this soup with love and you will be administering a hug!

RIPPA - PEASANT SOUP WITH SAUERKRAUT, BARLEY & SAUSAGE

This is more than just a soup. It's thick, hearty and is actually a 'meal-in-a bowl'. My Croatian Grandma used to make this soup. The aromas alone bring back wonderful memories.

Serves 6-8

My theory of soup making is the 'One Pot' and 'No Extra Steps'.
Just throw everything in and hope for the best.
And just watch what delicious results you'll get!

Add to a 10-12 quart stock pot:

1 16-24 oz.	Can or bag of SAUERKRAUT
1 lb.	SMOKED SAUSAGE, cut up into bite size pieces
1/2 lb.	HAM, cut up
11/2 cup	BARLEY, not cooked
2	ONIONS, chopped
2 cloves	GARLIC, minced
1-2	HAM BONES or Ham Hocks
2	BAY LEAVES
2 tsps.	THYME, dry
1 tsp.	LIQUID SMOKE

Add enough WATER to go about 4"-5" over the top of ingredients.
Bring to boil. Lower heat.
Cover and simmer for about 1 hour, stirring occasionally.
You can actually let this simmer for hours. Add more water as necessary so it's not too thick.

If you like MUSHROOMS, (1-2 cups sliced) throw some in now.
Simmer for 20 minutes. Adjust seasonings.
Skim any grease before serving.

Serve with crusty bread.

ANTIQUAN
PEPPERPOT SOUP/STEW

This is a soup with flavors compared to none, due to the unusual combinations of foods such as eggplant, squash, coconut, spinach, okra, corned beef, smoked pork and more.
And you know what? It works! It's delicious!

Serves 10-12

Add to a large stock pot:

1/2 lb.	CORNED BEEF BRISKET or Beef Brisket, cut into 1" cubes
1 small	EGGPLANT, cut up into 1/2" cubes (peeling is optional)
1/2 lb.	KALE, washed and chopped (using the stems adds fiber)
10 oz.	Package frozen OKRA or fresh, cut up
1/2 lb.	SMOKED PORK BUTT or SHOULDER, cut into 1" cubes
1 cup	GREEN ONIONS, chopped
1/2 lb.	BUTTERNUT SQUASH, peeled and cut into 1/2" cubes
1/2 lb.	ZUCCHINI, cut into 1/2" cubes
2 cloves	GARLIC, minced
8 cups	CHICKEN BROTH

Bring to boil. Reduce heat and simmer 1 to 1 1/2 hours, or until meat is tender.
Stir, adding:

4 cups	COCONUT MILK
4 tbsp.	TOMATO PASTE
1/2 tsp.	SAGE, dry
1/2 tsp.	THYME, dry
	SALT & PEPPER to taste

Simmer for about 1 hour until it has slightly thickened, stirring occasionally.
Add:

2 cups	PEAS, fresh or frozen

Cook 5 more minutes and serve up ladles & ladles of this beautiful soup.
Adjust seasonings to suit your tastes.

Don't forget to serve it with plenty of bread or cornbread to soak up all that goodness. You will love making this hearty stew like soup.

BEEF COGNAC STEW IN PUMKIN SHELLS

All this goodness is served in individual pumpkin shells. A stunning presentation!

THE STEW

Add to a large stock pot:

2 tbsps.	OLIVE OIL
1 medium	ONION, chopped
3 cloves	GARLIC, minced
2 lbs.	BEEF, lean shoulder or round - cut into 1" cubes

Saute until meat is browned on all sides.
Add:

1 lb.	SWEET POTATOES, peeled and cubed
1 lb.	White POTATOES, scrubbed and cubed
1 small	BUTTERNUT SQUASH, peeled and cubed
2	CARROTS, peeled and thickly sliced
2 small	ZUCCHINI, thickly sliced
1 stalk	CELERY, cut up
1 cup	Pitted PRUNES, cut in half
1/2 cup	Pitted DATES, cut in half
1/2 cup	Dried APRICOTS, cut in half
2/3 cup	COGNAC
3 tbsps.	BROWN SUGAR
2	BAY LEAVES
1/2 tsp.	THYME, dry
	Enough BEEF STOCK or water to cover
	SALT and PEPPER to taste

Bring to boil, reduce heat and simmer for about 1 to 1-1/2 hours, until vegetables are tender. Stir occasionally. While stew is cooking, prepare the pumpkins.

THE PUMPKINS

Serves 6

Use 6 PIE PUMPKINS. These are small pumpkins that have a rich orange color.
* Cut off tops about one third of the way down. It helps to cut a notch so it will be easier to replace the lid.
* Scrape seeds from lid and hollow out the insides.
* To each of the pumpkins add:

1 pat	BUTTER
1 tsp.	BROWN SUGAR
1 tsp.	COGNAC
Dash	SALT

* Place lids back on and place in baking pans.
Bake in 375ºF oven for about 45-60 min. until tender and can be pierced with a fork.
They should be firm enough to hold stew.

Do not over cook to the point of collaspe.

ASSEMBLING

When the STEW is done, thicken with:

2 tbsps.	CORNSTARCH mixed with
1/4 cup	SHERRY, Madeira Wine

* Pour into stew in thin stream while stirring.
If you want it thicker, repeat the above proceedure. Correct seasonings.
To assemble, place each pumpkin in a shallow soup dish.
* Carefully remove lids. Keep lids near their respective pumpkin so as not mix them up.
* Leave the juices that have collected in the bottom.
* Fill each pumpkin with the stew and place on the lids.
* To make an even more attractive presentation, place the bowls on plates and garnish with fall leaves.

Serve with warm bread or biscuits.

59

LAMB LENTIL STEW

This is a hearty stew with a taste of the Mediterranean.

Serves 8-12

Add to a lightly oiled stock pot, over medium heat:

3 lbs.	LAMB - fat trimmed, cut up into bite size chunks
1 large	ONION, cut up
2 cloves	GARLIC, minced

Saute, stirring occasionally, until meat is browned on all sides.

Add:

2-3 stalks	CELERY, cut up
4	CARROTS, cut up
3-4	POTATOES, cut up - not peeled
1 large	Can of stewed TOMATOES, with juices
2 qts.	WATER
3/4 cups	LENTILS, uncooked
4	BEEF BOUILLON Cubes
2 tsps.	THYME, dry
2 tsps.	OREGANO, dry
1	BAY LEAF
	SALT & PEPPER to taste

Optional: Adding lamb bones to the stock will enhance the flavor.

Bring to a boil. Reduce heat and simmer for 1 1/2 - 2 hours.

Adjust seasonings to suit your tastes.
You might want to add a little bit of red wine.

Skim off fat.
A good way to do this is to refrigerate it overnight and then spoon off the solidified fat.

Serve hot accompanied with lots of crusty bread.

HAWAIIAN PORTUGUESE SOUP

This soup is cultivated by the blending of cultures. Spicy food lovers and Island goers will love its distinctive flavor. It is hearty and spicy, so try this one on for size instead of chili.

Serves 6-8

Add to a large 8 qt. pot:

2 cups dried mixed	BEANS, washed and sorted
Enough	WATER to come up 2" over beans

Let soak overnight.

Or, bring to rapid boil for 10 minutes. Cover, turn off heat and let sit for at least one hour.

Add to the beans:

6 cups	BEEF STOCK
3/4 lb.	HAM BONES

Bring to boil, reduce heat and simmer for about 11/2 hours.

Add:

1-2 lbs.	SPICY SAUSAGE or Portuguese Linguica or Chorizo
4 cloves	GARLIC, minced
3 cups	RED POTATOES, cut up
2 cups	CARROTS, cut up
2 cups	ONIONS, cut up
2 cups	TOMATOES, fresh, cut up or canned diced
1 cup	CELERY, cut up
1/2 cup	PAPAYA JUICE
1 tsp. each	GINGER, CHILI PEPPER, THYME, PAPRIKA
	Favorite HOT SAUCE to taste
	SALT and PEPPER to taste

Simmer for 1-11/2 hours.

The aroma that fills the room will beckon you to taste.
Go ahead and then adjust the seasonings to your liking.

Garnish with papaya slices and serve with an Hawaiian sweet bread.

PASTA SAUCES

Versatile & Forgiving

Versatile,
because they go over a
variety of foods.

Forgiving,
because they will cover
up mistakes!

Pinot~Shiitake
Mushroom Sauce

*Pinot Grigio is a white Italian wine that is as good in a dish as
it is with it. The wine makes it a most flavorful sauce.*

Makes about 3 cups

Add to a sauté pan, over medium heat:

2 tbsps.	BUTTER or Olive Oil
1/2 cup	SHALLOTS, sliced or onion, chopped
	(Chopped Leeks also add a wonderful flavor.)
1/8 cup	PARSLEY, chopped
2 tbsps.	LEMON GRASS, chopped
	or 1 tbsp. grated lemon peel
1 clove	GARLIC, minced
12-16 oz.	SHITAKE MUSHROOMS, sliced
1/2 tsp. each	ROSEMARY and THYME, dry

Sauté for 3-5 minutes.

Sprinkle with:

      1 1/2 tbsps. FLOUR

Stir. Sauté a couple minutes.

Add, stirring:

    1/2 cup   CHICKEN STOCK, fresh or canned or you can use mushroom stock made from a dried mushroom powder available from gourmet stores or imported food wholesale supply houses.

    1 1/2 cups PINOT GRIGIO WINE - You can vary the flavor of this sauce by using different wines: Pinot Noir, Merlot, Marsala, Dry Vermouth, etc.

Bring to a boil. Simmer for about 15 minutes, stirring frequently.
Serve hot. Optional: garnish with fresh chopped rosemary.

Serve over meats, poultry, seafood, eggs, vegetables, rice, pasta or polenta

Hot Italian Sausage Cacciatori

Peppers, onions and mushrooms give this cacciatori real body.

Serves 6-8

Add to a large Dutch Oven or stock pot, over medium heat:

3 lb.	Hot ITALIAN SAUSAGE or a spicy Turkey Sausage, cut up
1 large	ONION, cut up
2	GREEN PEPPERS, sliced
8 oz	MUSHROOMS, cut into quarters or halves, depending on size. If they are small, leave whole.
1-3 cloves	GARLIC, minced
8-10	Fresh PLUM TOMATOES, chopped or 1 can plum tomatoes, using the liquid
1 can	TOMATO PASTE
1 can	RED WINE - use the tomato paste can, using the wine to get out the remainder of the tomato paste.
1/2 tsp. each	ROSEMARY, BASIL, THYME and OREGANO, dry SALT, PEPPER and Hot Sauce to taste

(If you like more sauce, add more tomatoes and adjust seasonings.)
Stir together, while cooking.
Bring to boil. Reduce heat and simmer for 1/2 - 1 hour.
Skim off the fat. Taste and adjust seasonings to your liking.

Serve over pasta, gnocchi, polenta, rice, or omlets. Don't forget the grated cheese.

Rabbit and Polenta

My Italian Grandma, Nona, would always make this. I would be underfoot in the kitchen watching her spin her magic. It was magic to see big smiles appear on faces. Truly a delicacy. Life is good...

Follow the above recipe. Use RABBIT or Chicken, instead of sausage.
Brown rabbit in the dutch oven. Cook on the stove or cover and slow cook in the oven at 350⁰ F. for 2 or more hours.
(Nona never made this with green peppers, but it's good either way.)
<u>Always</u> serve this over "POLENTA" (p. 101). It's the best!

Harrise Davidson's

Goat Cheese & Portabello Mushroom Sauce

When Harrise Davidson of Harrise Davidson Talent Agency, made this sauce, it was an instant addiction. To satisfy the craving, I had to immediately write a recipe for it. The goat cheese gives this sauce a most wonderfully distinct flavor. It is so delicious, I also wrote it as a recipe for bisque.
(See page 52)

Makes about 6 cups

Add to a medium saucepan over medium heat:

4 - 6 tbsps.	BUTTER
2/3 cup	LEEKS, thinly sliced
1/2 cup	ONIONS, chopped
1/2 cup	CELERY, chopped
1-2 cloves	GARLIC, minced or thinly sliced
3 cups	PORTABELLO MUSHROOMS, cut up

Sauté 10 - 20 minutes, until vegetables are tender, stirring occasionally. (Cook with the lid on to keep the juices from evaporating.)

Add:

1 cup	CHICKEN STOCK
1 cup	DRY VERMOUTH or dry white wine
1 tsp.	CHICKEN BOUILLON
1 tsp.	ROSEMARY, dry leaf, crumbled or 2 tsp. fresh, chopped
1/2 tsp.	THYME, dry or 1 tsp. fresh, chopped
	SALT & PEPPER to taste

Bring to a boil. Reduce heat and simmer for 10 - 15 minutes, uncovered.
Add while stirring:

1 cup	GOAT CHEESE that has been softened in the microwave and stirred until smooth.

Heat thoroughly. Avoid boiling. This will cause the sauce to curdle.
If making ahead, reheat on low heat or in the microwave to prevent scorching.

Serve over pasta, rice, potaoes, polenta, omelets, meats, fish and poultry.

Pumpkin Brandy Sauce

*When Autumn arrives and there is a nip in the air, serve this
rich delicious pasta sauce. It is a perfect fall dish.
This recipe makes a good size batch*

Makes about 8 cups

Add to a large sauce pan, over medium heat:
4-6 tbsps.	BUTTER
1 1/2 cups	ONION, chopped
1 cup	CELERY, chopped
1-2 cloves	GARLIC, minced

Sauté until vegetables are soft and tender and turn a carmelized color.

2 cups	Pureed PUMPKIN, cooked or canned (You can also use butternut squash.)
2 cups	Pureed SWEET POTATOES, cooked or canned
3 cups	HALF & HALF or Milk
1 cup	CREAM
1/3 cup	BROWN SUGAR
2 tsps.	MOLASSES
1 tsp.	MACE
1/2 tsp. each	ALLSPICE & NUTMEG
	SALT & PEPPER to taste

Stir until combined.
Cook over low heat until it comes to a boil. Avoid letting it overcook.
Stir frequently to prevent scorching. Remove from heat.

Add:
2/3 cup	BRANDY (Feel free to use more or less, depending on your tastes.)
3/4 cup	PARMESAN CHEESE

Adjust seasonings to your tastes.

❖❖❖❖❖❖❖❖

*Light Version: Omit butter and parmesan cheese. Substitute skim milk for creams.
Thicken with 2 T. cornstarch in 1/4 C. water.*

Broccoli - Gorgonzola Sauce

It's amazing how many people love this sauce. This Panozzo's Cafe favorite was served over omelets as well as pasta.

Makes about 6 cups

Steam:

　　　1 bunch　　　BROCCOLI, cut up

Steam a few minutes until barely tender, but do not over cook. Broccoli should keep its nice green color. A pinch of baking soda added to the water helps do this.

Drain and set aside while you make the GORGONZOLA SAUCE

Gorgonzola Sauce

Add to a 2 quart sauce pan over medium heat:

　　　4 - 6 tbsps.　　BUTTER
　　　1/2 cup　　　ONIONS, chopped
　　　1/2 cup　　　CELERY, chopped
　　　1-2 heads　　ROASTED GARLIC Paste

Sauté until vegetables are tender.

Add:

Roasted Garlic

Roast heads of garlic in a 37⁰ F. oven for about 45-60 minutes or until tender.
When done, let cool.
Cut in half lengthwise and squeeze out paste.

　　　11/2 cups　　CHICKEN STOCK
　　　1/2 cup　　　DRY VERMOUTH or dry white wine
　　　1 tsp.　　　CHICKEN BOUILLON
　　　1 tsp.　　　ROSEMARY, dry leaf, crumbled or 2 tsp. fresh, chopped
　　　1/2 tsp.each DILL & FENNEL, dry
　　　Dash　　　HOT SAUCE
　　　　　　　　SALT & PEPPER to taste

Bring to a boil. Reduce heat and simmer for 10 - 15 minutes, uncovered.

Add while stirring:

　　　1 -11/2 cups GORGONZOLA CHEESE that has been crumbled
　　　1/2 cup　　　Grated PARMESAN CHEESE
　　　1 cup　　　Heavy CREAM or Half & Half

If using Half & Half, you may need to thicken sauce with 2 T. cornstarch mixed in 1/4 cup of water.

Heat thoroughly. Avoid boiling. This will cause the sauce to curdle.

Stir in broccoli just before serving so it keeps it color.

If making ahead, reheat on low heat or in the microwave to prevent scorching.

FROM BRUNCHES TO DINNER

These are comfort foods,
so gather your family...
gather your friends...
&
Enjoy!

MAIN DISHES

BRUNCH PASTA SHELLS

Pasta lovers will enjoy this dish. The shells are filled with eggs, leeks, mushrooms and havarti cheese. Read the recipe a few times to understand the concept, then go ahead and create!

Serves 6-8

Add to a large skillet or wok over medium heat:

2 tbsps.	CORN OIL or Butter
1 stalk	LEEK, washed and chopped
1 cup	MUSHROOMS, sliced
1-2 cloves	GARLIC, minced

Saute, stirring occasionally until vegetables are tender, 10-20 minutes.
Add:

6 cups	Beaten EGGS or egg whites for less fat
1/4 cup	DRY VERMOUTH
1/2 tsp.	Dry THYME
	SALT & PEPPER to taste

Cook, stirring constantly until eggs are cooked, scramble-style.
Have the following items ready and assembled:

	Lightly oiled 13" by 9" baking dish
16-24 large	PASTA SHELLS, cook in boiling water with 2 T. oil and drain
	* You'll want to cook extra to make up for ones that get damaged.
1 cup	CREAM or Half & Half or (Skim Milk for less fat)
1 cup	HAVARTI CHEESE, grated (use less cheese to decrease fat)
	Swiss or Gryere can also be substituted.

TO ASSEMBLE:

1. Pour 1/2 cup of cream in the bottom of the baking dish.
2. Fill shells with egg mixture and place side by side in baking dish. Fill enough shells to fit snuggly in the pan. Depending on the size of the shells, if you need more eggs, scramble a few more. Season with salt, pepper, & herbs.
3. Top with cheese.
4. Drizzle with the rest of the cream.
5. Bake at 375°F for 25-35 minutes or until bubbly and golden brown.

A perfect accompaniment to this is "Spicy Herb Onion Bread". See 'Breads'.

EGG STRUDEL WITH WILD MUSHROOMS

When you need something special for a brunch, this is as delicious as it is elegant. Also perfect for a late supper.

Serves 4-6

Have prepared and assembled:

2 cups	Scrambled EGGS, seasoned with salt and pepper or use an egg substitute
17 1/4 oz.	Pkg. frozen PUFF PASTRY, thawed
	Roll out on floured surface and cut out 2 sheets approximately 14" by 6"
1/2 cup	CHEESE, grated - Muenster, Havarti or Swiss
1/8 cup	BREAD CRUMBS
1/4 cup	DRY VERMOUTH
1	EGG WHITE beaten with 1 teaspoon water
	SAUTED WILD MUSHROOMS, recipe follows

SAUTÉD WILD MUSHROOMS

Add to a large skillet over medium heat:

2-4 tbsps.	BUTTER
2 cups	MUSHROOMS, sliced - Shiitake, Portabello, Oyster, Crimini, Morels, Button, etc. - take your pick
1/2 cup	LEEKS or Green Onions, chopped
1-2	Cloves GARLIC, minced
1/2 tsp.	Dry ROSEMARY or 1 teaspoon fresh - chopped
1/4 cup	DRY VERMOUTH
	SALT & PEPPER to taste

Sauté until mushrooms and leeks are tender, about 10-20 minutes.

TO ASSEMBLE:

1. Line a cookie sheet with parchment paper.
2. Place a sheet of puff pastry on it.
3. Sprinkle with bread crumbs.
4. Place eggs on it leaving a 1/2" border on all sides.
5. Top with mushrooms.
6. Sprinkle with cheese.
7. Brush edges with water
8. Place 2nd puff pastry on top.
9. Press edges to seal.
10. Make vent cuts*

Brush the top with egg white that has been beaten with 1 tsp. of water.
Option: Sprinkle with sesame or celery seeds.
Bake in preheated 375°F. oven for about 30-45 minutes or until golden brown. Serve hot.
*To make vent cuts, use a scissors, snip a row of "V's", about 1" apart, on the top crust to allow the steam to escape. You can also make cut outs using aspic cutters. Do before placing on top.

71

BRUNCH LASAGNA
OF SPINACH & GORGONZOLA

*Need something delicious? Something different for a crowd? Consider this
one and watch the smiles.*

Serves 6-8

Add to a large mixing bowl:

6-8 cups	Scrambled EGGS - scramble in olive oil, salt and pepper to taste (Use egg whites for less fat content)
3 cups	Frozen, chopped SPINACH, thawed. Squeeze to drain. or fresh spinach, steamed, chopped and drained.
2 medium	ONIONS, chopped and sauted in a little olive oil
2 tsps.	ROSEMARY LEAVES, dry, crumbled
2 tsps.	DILL WEED, dry
1 tsps.	OREGANO, dry
1 tsps.	BASIL, dry
	SALT & PEPPER to taste
	Enough BREAD CRUMBS to absorb any excess liquid

Have the following items ready and assembled:

	Lightly oiled Lasagna Pan
12-15	LASAGNA noodles, cooked & drained
2-3	TOMATOES, sliced
2 cups	GORGONZOLA, crumbled
1-11/2cups	CREAM or Half & Half (Skim Milk for less fat stirred with 2 T.Cornstarch)
1 cup	ASIAGO, Parmesan &/or Romano cheeses, grated
1/3 cup	BREAD CRUMBS

TO ASSEMBLE:

1. Pour enough cream into the lasagna pan to cover the bottom.
2. Layer in this order: You can do 2 or 3 layers. Divide ingredients accordingly
      Noodles - Egg/Spinach mixture - Tomatoes - Bread Crumbs - Gorgonzola -
      Asiago - Cream
3. Repeat
Sprinkle top with chopped walnuts, dry rosemary and a pinch of cayenne.
Bake at 375°F, uncovered, about 30-45 minutes, until golden & bubbly.

SPINACH LASAGNA FOR A CROWD

Fridays meant Pasta Night at Panozzo's Cafe. This is one of the dishes guests would always look for and then come back for seconds. So make lots, which this recipe allows you to do!

serves 12-16

Cook the LASAGNA NOODLES while making the FILLING (recipe follows).

1 1/2 lb.	LASAGNA NOODLES (25-30 noodles)

Drop noodles in several quarts of boiling water. Salt to taste.
Cook aldente (do not over cook). Drain. Rinse.
Drizzle with OLIVE OIL to prevent sticking. Cover.

SPINACH FILLING

Add to a large mixing bowl:

2 lbs.	Frozen, chopped SPINACH - thawed. Squeeze out excess liquid			
5 lbs.	RICOTTA CHEESE	1-3 cloves	GARLIC, minced
2	EGGS, beaten	2 tbsps.	VINEGAR
1 cup	Grated, PARMESAN CHEESE		or Vermouth
1/2 cup	ONION, minced	2 tbsps. each	OREGANO & DILL
Dash	HOT SAUCE	1 tsp.	FENNEL, dry
	SALT & PEPPER to taste	Optional:	1 C. grated Carrots

Mix together until well combined.

Preheat oven to 375° F. Assemble the following:

	Cooked LASAGNA NOODLES
	SPINACH FILLING
1 1/2 lbs.	MOZZARELLA CHEESE, grated
1 cup	Grated PARMESAN CHEESE
13-16 cups	Favorite PASTA SAUCE
1 large	LASAGNA PANS: 16" x 11" x 2 1/2 " or 14" x 10" x 4" - oiled
	or 2 smaller baking pans (oiled). This way you can freeze one!

Here is one way to assemble lasagna in layers:

1st. PASTA SAUCE 1/4" thick in bottom of pan(s).	4th. MOZZARELLA
2nd. LASAGNA NOODLES (dble layer) paint with sauce	5th. PARMESAN
3rd. SPINACH FILLING	6th. Repeat

End up with an extra layer of noodles & sauce on the top. This prevent the cheeses from burning.
Cover with foil. Can be frozen at this point. Bake frozen for 2 1/2 - 3 hr.
Bake about 1 1/2 hours or more. (Line oven rack with foil to catch drips.) Uncover and bake 10-15 minutes more, topping with a bit more cheeses, if you wish. It is ready when it is hot and bubbly. Let rest for 10 minutes before serving, so it slices better and doesn't run.

If you make it up ahead & refrigerated it, be sure to increase cooking time.

73

SPINACH RICOTTA ROLLS

Using the recipe for "Spinach Lasagna for a Crowd" on the previous recipe page, this is lasagna in a different form. Instead of layering, you are rolling.

To make:
Lay out a lasagna noodle and fill one end with 1 or 2 tablespoons of filling.

Roll up & set in pan filled with 1/2" pasta sauce.

You can lay rolls down, seam side down, or set them up in pan.

Repeat until pan is full.

Top with cheeses & pasta sauce or a cream sauce.

Cover & bake 1-11/2 hrs. Uncover for last 15 minutes of baking.

Let rest 10-15 minutes before serving. This gives them a chance to firm up.

SPINACH RICOTTA OMELETS

This makes a delicious supper as well as a morning booster!

Make omelets.

Use left over filling, cheese & sauce from the *"Spinach Lasagna for a Crowd"* to fill omlets.

Top with sauce & cheeses.

Put in oven or under broiler until cheese melts.

Most yummy!

SCHOOLHOUSE SHOP

PASTA WITH SHRIMP

This is a creation of Roy Krezik and Jim Ruge, owners of the Schoolhouse Shop in Chesterton, Indiana. They blend gourmet products with fresh ingredients to come up with this delicious dish.

It involves very specific gourmet items, available in gourmet shops and Panozzo's Pantry in the Schoolhouse Shop. (219 926.1551)

Serves 2-4

Cook in plenty of boiling, salted water, until aldente:

1 bag	Castellana PASTA (Foglie D'Oliva -spinach pasta in the shape of olive leaves)

Drain, drizzle with olive oil and keep warm.

Heat in saucepan:

1 16oz. jar	Patsy's VODKA SAUCE or a great Marinara sauce

Keep on low until ready to serve.

While the pasta is cooking and the sauce is heating, saute the shrimp:

SAUTÉD SHRIMP

Sauté together:

2 tbsps.	BUTTER
2 tbsps.	Extra Virgin OLIVE OIL
4 tbsps.	SHALLOTS, chopped
2 cloves	GARLIC, minced
1 lb.	Fresh SHRIMP, shelled & veined

Cook just until shrimp turn pink. Do not over cook.

While still over heat, you can give it a splash of:

DRY VERMOUTH or dry white wine

"PLATING IT" meaning to make up a plate of it for serving:

Scoop enough pasta to cover two-thirds of the plate.
Ladle some pasta sauce over the pasta.
Fill the other third of the plate with some the sauted shrimp and it's juices.
Garnish the entire plate with fresh chopped flat leaf parsley & grated or shaved cheese.

Use warmed plates for "plating" and be sure to cover and keep warm while assembling the others.

MEATBALLS WITH FRESH FENNEL

This one is for my dear sister Marie, who absolutely loves meatballs. Also, thanks to Bill and Lynda Stone, who inspired me to come up with a killer recipe because of a certain recipe contest. We did it!

Add to a large mixing bowl:

1 1/2 lbs.	GROUND BEEF
1/2 lb.	ITALIAN SAUSAGE, out of casing
1/2 lb.	GROUND LAMB
2/3 cup	FRESH FENNEL, finely chopped
1/4 cup	Fresh MINT, finely chopped or dry
1/4 cup	Fresh BASIL, finely chopped or 2 teaspoon dry
2 tbsps.	Fresh ROSEMARY, finely chopped or 2 teaspoon dry
2 tbsps.	Fresh DILL, finely chopped or 2 teaspoons dry
1/2 cup	ONION, finely chopped
1/2 cup	CELERY, finely chopped
1-3 cloves	GARLIC, minced
1/3 cup	Smoky BBQ SAUCE or regular BBQ sauce plus 1 teaspoon liquid smoke
1 cup	BREAD CRUMBS
1/2 cup	PARMESAN or Romano Cheese
2	EGGS, beaten
2 tbsps.	BALSAMIC VINEGAR or Cider Vinegar
2 tbsps.	RED WINE
2 tbsps.	WORCESTERSHIRE
Dashes	HOT SAUCE, SALT & PEPPER to taste

Using your hands, mix together until ingredients are well combined.
Shape into balls using about 1/4 cup mixture per meatball.

Pour your favorite tomato sauce into 2 baking pans, filling half full.
Suggestion: Add 1-2 CUP chopped fresh FENNEL or 1-2 tablespoons dry fennel to your sauce to enhance the flavor of it and the meatballs.

Arrange raw meatballs in both pans. Pour more sauce over to cover them.

Cover and bake at 375⁰ F. for 1 to 1 1/2 hours until meatballs are firm.
Sauce will be bubbly. Skim the grease. These can be made and cooked days in advance.
Avoid using aluminum pans. Reheat covered until hot & bubbly.

Serve over polenta, gnocchi or your favorite pasta.

BILL SWINDLE'S
POT ROAST

This is THE most delicious pot roast ever! It is hearty yet simple. Put it on the stove and forget about it, if you can.
The aromas will have you peeking under the lid for a quick whiff and little taste.

Servers 6-10

6-7 lb.	BEEF ROAST

Rub with:

| 1 tbsp. | ROSEMARY, dry |
| 1-3 cloves | GARLIC, minced |

Dust with flour.

In a heavy 12-quart stock pot, brown the meat on all sides in:

| 4-6 tbsp. | OLIVE OIL |

Add:

2 cups	BEEF CONSUME, stock or broth
1 1/2 cups	Red WINE
2 cups	TOMATOES-stewed (16oz can of Tomatoes)
2	BAY LEAVES
6 whole	CLOVES
1 tsp.	CINNAMON

Simmer covered, over low heat for 1 1/2 hours.

Add:

4-6 small	ONIONS, cleaned and left whole
1 stalk	CELERY, cut up
8-12	New RED POTATOES, left whole
6-8	CARROTS, cut into large pieces
1/2 lb.	MUSHROOMS, whole
	SALT, PEPPER & HOT SAUCE to taste

Simmer covered another 1/2 hour.

Remove vegetables & set aside.

Increase heat & stir in cornstarch mixture to thicken:

| 2 tbsp. | CORNSTARCH in | 1/2 CUP WATER |

Add:

| 1/2 cup | HORSERADISH |
| | Cooked VEGETABLES from above |

Slice meat and serve with vegetables.

All you need is lots of crusty bread and IT'S A MEAL! Salad may have to be served as the second course because everyone will be anxious to dig in!

CINCINATTI CHILI *5 WAY*

This is, by far, a most unique tasting chili. Once you adapt a taste for it, you'll be craving it. And nothing tops a hot dog better than this!

Serves 8-10

Add to a 4-6 quart stock pot:

    2 lbs.   GROUND BEEF

    3 cups   WATER or Beef Stock

Cook, stirring, until the meat has loosened to a fine texture, about 30 minutes.

Add:

4 medium	ONIONS, chopped	2 tbsps.	WORCESTERSHIRE
3 cloves	GARLIC, minced	1 tbsp.	OREGANO, dry
1 large	Can TOMATOES	3	BAY LEAVES
5 tbsps.	CHILI POWDER	2 tsps.	CINNAMON
4 tbsps.	COCOA POWDER	2 tsps.	ALLSPICE
4 tbsps.	WHITE VINEGAR	2 tsps.	TOBASCO
2 tbsps.	CUMIN		SALT to taste

Stir to blend.

Bring to a boil. Reduce heat and simmer for 2 1/2 - 3 hours. Pot may be covered for last hour of cooking after the desired consistency is reached. Skim off fat.

Have assembled: Cooked spaghetti, shredded colby cheese, chopped yellow onion, & kidney beans, then take your pick of the following ways.

5 Way
Spaghetti, Chili, Cheese, Onion & Beans
4 Way
Spaghetti, Chili, Cheese & Onion
3 Way
Spaghetti, Chili & Cheese
2 Way
Spaghetti & Chili
Don't forget the SOUR CREAM for added goodness.

The chili can be refrigerated overnight so the fat can easily be removed off the top.

LIFE'S A BOWL OF
CHERRY MEATLOAF

A long time comfort food with a twist. Dried Cherries are ground up and added to the meatloaf to give it a little rosy redness after it is cooked. It is also great way to keep the fat content down, making it an upscale, hometown favorite. Let's make a good size batch so there's plenty leftover to slice for SANDWICHES! Yeah!

In warm water to cover:

    1 cup   DRIED CHERRIES

Soak for about 15 minutes until they have plumped. Drain, but don't squeeze dry. Put in a food processor and process until coarsely ground.

Transfer CHERRIES to large mixing bowl and add:

3 lbs.	Lean GROUND BEEF
1 cup	BREAD CRUMBS or Rolled Oats
1/2 cup	ONION, finely copped
1/2 cup	FENNEL - bulb part, finely chopped
1/2 cup	PARSLEY, chopped
2 cloves	GARLIC, chopped
1 tbsp.	MADEIRA, Sherry, or Port Wine
1	EGG, beaten
	SALT & PEPPER to taste

Mix until thoroughly combined. Shape into 1 large loaf. Transfer to a baking dish. Bake in preheated 350° for about 1 hour. It should be firm to the touch and juices run clear.

Serve with "Wasabi Mashed Potatoes". (See "Side Dishes")

CHERRY MEATLOAF PIES

This is a nice presentation for the Cherry Meatloaf. It gives it a Cherry Pie look.

Makes 2 pies

Divide prepared meatloaf mixture in half. Press each into an 8" or 9" pie pan.

Bake in a preheated 350° F for about 30 minutes. Pour off excess grease.

Top each with a prepared pie crust. Crimp edges. Brush with milk.

Cut slits in the top. Sprinkle with celery seeds, sesame seeds or ground nuts and parmesan cheese.

Or, using a pastry bag, pipe mashed potatoes on the top to resemble a lattice.

Return to oven and bake for about 20-30 minutes more, until golden brown. Remove from oven and let it rest 10 minutes.

ALEX PANOZZO'S

ROASTED LEG OF LAMB

WITH COFFEE HONEY GLAZE

My brother receives many praises whenever he serves this meal. The Coffee Honey Glaze has a distinctive taste that uniquely compliments the lamb, like nothing else!

Serves 6-8

Add to a medium mixing bowl:
- 2 cups   COFFEE, strongly brewed
- 1/2 cup   HONEY
- 1/4 cup   ORANGE MARMALADE
- 1/2 tsp.   CINNAMON
- 1/4 tsp.   ALLSPICE

Stir together.

Place on a rack in a shallow roasting pan:
- 1 leg of   LAMB, about 5 lbs.

Roast in oven at 325^0 F. for 2 1/2 - 3 hours,
or until meat thermometer registers 175^0-180^0 depending on your desired degree of doneness.

Baste with coffee mixture frequently during the roasting's period.

When lamb is done, remove from roasting pan.
Transfer drippings to saucepan.

Make a thickening agent by mixing together;
- 4 tbsps.   FLOUR
- 1/4 cup   WATER

Stir until smooth.

Cook drippings over low heat. Stir while gradually adding flour mixture.
Cook stirring constantly until thickened.

Serve thickened glaze over sliced lamb.

COUSCOUS WITH EGGPLANT

Couscous is a pasta. Once you start using it you will discover how versatile, quick and handy it is.

You could serve this as a side dish, but as not to underestimate it, try serving it as a vegetarian main course.

Serves 4 - 8

Add to a large skillet, over medium heat:

2 tbsps.	OLIVE OIL
1 cup	GREEN ONIONS, chopped
1 small	ONION, chopped
2 cloves	GARLIC, minced
1 large	EGGPLANT, cut into 1/4" cubes, unpeeled- about 4 cups.
1 tsp. each:	CORIANDER, CUMIN, OREGANO, dry
1/2 tsp.	SALT and PEPPER to taste

Sauté, stirring occasionally, until eggplant is tender.

Add:

  2 cups   WATER, Vegetable or Chicken Stock
Bring to a boil.

Add:

  2 cups   COUSCOUS
Cook about 5 minutes or until couscous starts to absorb the liquids.
Cover and turn off heat. Let sit 10 minutes. Stir to fluff couscous.

Add juice and rind of 1 LEMON.

If you like, drizzle with a little extra virgin OLIVE OIL.

Stir and serve. Garnish with chopped green onions or chopped parsley.

Optional: Serve with a side of plain yogurt.

AS A SALAD...

After cooking it, sprinkle with vinegar and chill.

Serve on gourmet greens. Garnish with tomato wedges.

81

PICADILLO, A CARIBBEAN BEEF HASH

This comes to you with help of my friend Carmen Cabrera, who really knows how to cook this up. In the Caribbean, this spicy hash is traditionally served for Saturday night supper. It is also used as a filling for enchiladas and tacos, even scrambled with eggs.

Serves 6-8

Soak   together:
1/2 cup	Dark RUM
1/2 cup	Dark RAISINS

Set aside.

Saute the following in the olive oil:
2 tbsps.	OLIVE OIL
2 lbs.	GROUND CHUCK or sirloin
1/2 lb.	Lean GROUND PORK
3 tbsps.	TOMATO PASTE

Brown meats, crumbling with spoon, about 5 minutes.
Drain excess fat.
Add:
1 large	ONION, finely chopped
1 large	GREEN BELL PEPPER, finely chopped
6 cloves	GARLIC, minced
1 small	Hot CHILI PEPPER, finely chopped

Saute until vegetables are tender, stirring occasionally.
Add:
2 large	TOMATOES, cored & chopped
1/2 tsp.	CINNAMON
1/2 tsp.	CLOVES (ground)
1 tbsp.	BALSAMIC VINEGAR
1 tbsp.	SUGAR
1 tbsp. each	OREGANO, CUMIN, CORIANDER, dry
2-3 tbsps.	Fresh CILANTRO, chopped
1/4 cup	GREEN OLIVES, Pimento-Stuffed
1 tbsp.	CAPERS - optional
1	BAY LEAF
1 cup	BEEF STOCK - fresh or canned
	The RUM & RAISINS

Simmer for about 45 minutes, stirring occasionally.

Serve with "White Rice Caribbean Style" p. 98, "Black Beans Caribbean Style", p. 99, "Fried Plantains", p. 97 or "Fried Sweet Potatoes", p. 97.

HOT & SPICY JERK
JAMAICAN BBQ SEASONING

This makes a great Father's Day gift. Whip up a batch for dad, then point him in the direction of the grill. Now watch him get all the praise.

Add to a food processor:

1 medium	RED ONION, chopped
1/4 cup	CHIVES, chopped
1 tsp.	THYME, dry
2 tbsps.	CORN OIL or Vegetable Oil
1 tsp.	ALLSPICE
1/4 tsp.	NUTMEG
1/2 tsp.	CINNAMON
1-5	HOT PEPPERS
	[Jalapeno or Chili peppers]
1/4 tsp.	BLACK PEPPER

Process until combined.

Refrigerate 2 hours or overnight.

Rub on meats, fish or veggies, then grill to perfection and ENJOY!

Keep this seasoning mix covered and stored in the refrigerator. It will keep for up to a week.

You can also use spoonfuls of this mixes an enhancer for soups, stews, sauces, salsas and salads. Once you get the hang of using it, you will always want to have a batch made up and on hand.

83

CRESPELLE (ITALIAN CRÊPES)

We know them as crêpes in France, but in Italy they are known to as crespelle. They are versatile and delectable.

Makes about 30

This is an express version of the traditional bowl method. For a sweet crespelle, add 2 tablespoons of sugar before blending.

To a blender or food processor, add:

4		EGGS
2 cups		MILK
1 3/4 cups		UNBLEACHED FLOUR
4 tbsps.		BUTTER, melted
1/4 tsp.		SALT

Blend well until very smooth. There should be no lumps.

Let the batter rest about 30 minutes. This will relax the batter, loosening the elasticity of the glutenous flour, allowing it to pour more easily and evenly.

Use a crêpe pan, a cast iron skillet or a non stick pan.
* I use a 9" non stick pan and have great success.

Heat over moderate to moderately high flame. The pan must be hot.
Adjust and keep the flame regulated throughout cooking of the crêpes.

Keep the pan greased with oil or butter throughout the cooking process.

Pour a thin layer of batter into the hot, greased skillet, quickly tilting the pan so the batter spreads evenly.
Crespelle should about 1/24" thin and practically transparent.
The first few hardly ever turn out. (They make good snacks dipped in preserves or a chocolate sauce.)

They cook very quickly, about 30 seconds.
Then flip the crêpe using a spatula or whatever works well for you. (To flip it in the air, be sure to loosen the edges first.)
After they're flipped, cook for 20-30 seconds.

Crespelle can be made up 3 days in advance. Make stacks of 5-10 and keep well wrapped in the refrigerator.

Use these to make "Asparagus & Smoked Salmon Crespelle" on the next page.

ASPARAGUS & SMOKED SALMON CRESPELLE (ITALIAN CRÊPES)

This is makes a beautiful dish for a dinner or luncheon. Easter brunch is also a perfect setting. Making these is merely a matter of assembling ingredients, which you can do well in advance.

Makes about 8 -10 filled crêpes

<u>CRESPELLES</u>	8-10 (crêpe) made using preceding recipe, or buy prepared crepes.
<u>ASPARAGUS</u>	Steam 24 - 32 stems of. (Be sure to wash & trim 1/4" off bottom.) Sprinkle with about 1 teaspoon <u>DILL WEED</u>.
<u>SHALLOTS</u>	Sauté 8 in about 2 tablespoons of <u>BUTTER</u>. Add approximately: 1 tbsp. <u>LEMON JUICE</u> and 1/4 cup <u>DRY VERMOUTH</u> Set aside and keep warm so butter stays melted.
<u>SMOKED SALMON</u>	Break up 1/2 lb-1lb into medium size pieces.
<u>Hard Boiled EGGS</u>	Slice up 8-10
<u>CREAM CHEESE</u>	Soften 8-12 oz.
<u>CAPERS</u> (Optional)	Drain a 3 oz. jar
<u>GRUYERE</u>	Grated to amount to 1-11/2 cups. (Swiss or Harvarti can be used.)
<u>BAKING DISH</u>	Butter a glass or ceramic baking dish, 15" x 93/4" (4 quart)
<u>HEAVY CREAM</u>	1/8-1/4 cup

Preheat oven at 375⁰ F.

TO ASSEMBLE

1. Lay a CRESPELLE (crêpe) down.
    Spread a heaping teaspoon of soft CREAM CHEESE down the center.
2. Lay in 3-4 stems of ASPARAGUS on cream cheese.
3. Continue to fill with desired amounts of:
    SMOKED SALMON, HARD BOILED EGGS, CAPERS, Salt & Pepper to taste.
4. Roll up and place seam down in buttered baking dish with cream.
5. Repeat until baking dish is snugly filled. (7-8 down & 2 vertically along the side.)
    Keep crepes close to each other so they don't get loose during baking.
6. Brush them with the shallot butter and drizzle remaining over all.
7. Pour HEAVY CREAM over top. (1/8-1/4 cup or however much you would like.)
8. Sprinkle with a little more salt, white pepper and dill weed.
9. Cover with foil.
10. Bake in 375⁰ F. oven for about 30 minutes.
11. Remove foil.
    Top with the GRATED CHEESE, spreading out evenly.
12. Continue to bake uncovered until cheese in melted and bubbly. 15-20 min.)
    Allow crespelle to rest for about 10 minutes before serving.

STUFFED CHILEAN SEA BASS WITH SHRIMP SAUCE

Tender forkfulls of shear bliss, is the best way to describe this dish.

Serves 4

Rinse and pat dry:

    2 large portions   CHILEAN SEA BASS (about 3-31/2 lbs)

With a sharp knife, slice each portion in half <u>horizontally</u>, like you would split a cake layer in half. The stuffing will go between these two layers.

Sprinkle each portion with a little:

    LEMON JUICE,   CUMIN,   TARRAGON,   SALT & PEPPER

STUFFING

To a sauté pan over medium high heat, melt:

    4 tbsps.   BUTTER

Add:

2 cups	chopped	MUSHROOMS
1 cup	chopped	CELERY
1/2 cup	diced	ONIONS
1/2 CUP	chopped	PARSLEY
1-2 cloves	minced	GARLIC
		SALT & PEPPER to taste

Sauté until barely tender.

(Half of this mixture will be used for the stuffing and the other half for the sauce.)

<u>Remove approximately HALF</u> the mixture to a bowl and add:

3 cups	cooked	WILD & BROWN RICE
2	beaten	EGGS
2 tbsps.	or more	sauterne (enough to moisten)

Mix well.

Place 2 potions of bass in buttered baking dish. Divide up stuffing and put on these. Top with the other 2 pieces.

Brush tops with melted BUTTER.

Bake in preheated 400° F. oven for 15 minutes. Cover and lower heat to 300° and continue to bake for 45 - 60 min. (Before covering you can give it a splash of Sauterne.)

Before removing Sea Bass from the oven, make the sauce.

SAUCE

To the sauté pan of vegetables, add:

    2 tbsps. heaping   FLOUR

Stir and cook for 30-60 seconds then add:

    11/2-2 cup   CLAM JUICE, Fish Stock or Milk

Bring to boil and add:

1/2 lb. small	SHRIMP, peeled and deveined
2-4 tbsps.	SAUTERNE
1/4-1/2 tsps. each	CUMIN & TARRAGON

Cook a few minutes until shrimp turns pink. Adjust seasonings . Salt & pepper to taste and a dash of hot sauce.

Cut the 2 stuffed bass in half to make 4 portions. Pour sauce over bass to serve.

86

SIDE DISHES

Never under estimate
this group.

They are strong in numbers.

Enough of them and
it's a meal!

Who needs a main course?

Notice, I didn't say
DESSERT!

Potatoes with an Attitude

These have a crunchy outer crust made with crumbled tortilla chips. They are spicy and satisfying.

Serves 4-6

Add to a bowl:

| 1 | EGG WHITE and whisk |

In another bowl add:

1-2 tbsps.	CORN OIL, or Vegetable Oil
1 cup	Crushed TORTILLA CHIPS
1/4 tsp. each	THYME, OREGANO, CAYENNE, CUMIN, & CHILI POWDER
1/8 tsp.	CURRY Powder

Mix together.

Slice 1/4" thick or in wedges:

| 4-6 | RED POTATOES, unpeeled |

Dip potatoes in egg whites, then in chip mix.

Repeat for an extra crunch. Sprinkle with salt and pepper.

Place on oiled baking sheet(s) in one layer.

Bake in a 400°F. oven for 30-45 minutes until browned and tender when pierced with a fork.

Note: Stir potatoes once or twice during roasting to ensure even browning.

Make extra to keep in the freezer for the kids!

After baking, let cool and store in air tight freezer bags. Reheat frozen in 400° oven on oiled cookie sheet. For easy clean up, line a cookie sheet with foil, and oil. Bake until crisp.

Potatoes with Leeks

*Being a lover of this vegetable, I could come up with
100 potato recipes alone. Here are a few more
for this versatile staple.*

Serves 4-8

Into a lightly oiled large baking dish, layer in <u>2 layers</u>, of the following:

4 lbs.(approx.)	RED POTATOES, raw unpeeled, sliced thin	
	Slice potatoes in water so they do not turn brown - Drain	
2 cups	LEEKS, chopped	
2 tsps.	THYME	
2 tsps.	ROSEMARY	
1 tsp.	SAVORY or Sage	
2 tbsps.	FLOUR	
2	BAY LEAVES	
	SALT & PEPPER to taste	

Heat together:

1 cup	CONSOMME, or chicken broth
1/2 cup	DRY VERMOUTH
1 cup	CREAM
5-6 oz.	GOAT CHEESE
2 tbsps.	BUTTER or Olive Oil

Heat gently until goat cheese melts. Do not boil.
Pour over the top of potatoes

Top with:

3/4 -1 cup	BREAD CRUMBS that have been tossed with 3 tablespoons melted butter or oil.

Cover and bake at 350°F. for 30-40 minutes or until tender and bubbly.

Remove cover and bake about 10 more minutes to let top brown.

*This dish cannot be made up ahead because potatoes that are exposed to oxygen
will turn color. You can however, boil potatoes first, then assemble.
Refrigerate over night and bake the next day, increasing baking time.*

Lemon Potatoes, Herbed & Roasted

Cut the potatoes in your favorite shape.
They are great as fries, wedges or chips.

Serves 6-8

Add to a bowl:

8-10 cups	RED POTATOES, cut into chunks, unpeeled
1 1/2 tbsp.	PARMESAN
2 tsps.	ROSEMARY
1 tsp.	BASIL
1 tsp.	THYME
2-4 tbsps.	Extra Virgin OLIVE OIL or Lemon Grapeseed Oil
1	LEMON, grated rind of
Juice of 1	LEMON
	SALT, PEPPER & Hot Sauce to taste

Toss together until well combined.

Place potatoes on a lightly oiled baking sheet or sheets.
Be sure potatoes are in a single layer.

Bake in a 400°F. oven for 30-45 minutes until browned and tender when pierced with a fork.

Note: Stir potatoes once or twice during roasting to ensure even browning.

Once cut, raw potatoes turn color, so these must be prepared and
then roasted right away. If you want to make these ahead of time roast them
and then reheat in the oven until crisp.

Shari Filoni's Favorite
Cafe Potatoes

At Panozzo's Cafe these were known as "Skillet Cheese Potatoes". With or without cheese Shari would have us top them in a variety of ways. Steamed veggies and poached eggs was a breakfast favorite.

Serves 6-8

Boil:

6-8 cups   RED POTATOES, cut into chunks

Do not over cook. Potatoes should not be mushy.

Drain.

Transfer to large oiled baking dish and add:

1/3 cup   OLIVE OIL or Corn Oil
2 tsps.   OREGANO, dry
1 tsp.   THYME, dry
            SALT & PEPPER to taste

Toss together until well combined.

Cover and bake at 375° F. for about 30-40 minutes until hot.

Optional:

Uncover and top with:

1-2 cups   COLBY or CHEDDAR CHEESE, grated

Return to oven until cheese is melted and bubbly.

Garnish with chopped green onions or chives before serving.

Wasabi Mashed Potatoes

These are mashed potatoes with a slight kick.
Just enough difference for taste buds to take notice.

Serves 4-6

Add to a medium stock pot:

4-6	White POTATOES, washed & cut up
	Do not peel. The skins give it texture.
	Red potatoes work well too. If using new red potatoes, use enough to make up 1 1/2 - 2 pounds.

Add enough water to cover.   Salt.

Option: Feel free to add 1 or 2 chicken bouillon cubes to enhance the flavor. If you do, be sure to decrease the amount of salt a bit.

Boil until very tender and somewhat mushy.

Drain well and put back in the same pot.

Add:

1-2 tbsps.	Prepared WASABI
1/3 cup	MILK or Cream, or Skim Milk, heated. If the potatoes are dry, add enough liquid to make them creamy.
2-4 tbsps.	Butter or Oil - optional
	SALT & PEPPER to taste

Mash potatoes. It's nice to keep them a little lumpy.
They will have a green tint. (Nice for St. Patrick's Day!)

Try adding roasted garlic for a variation.
Prepared HORSERADISH can be used instead of Wasabi, to give it a kick, but without the green tint.

Roasted Garlic

Roast heads of garlic in a 375° F. oven for about 45-60 minutes or until tender. When done, let cool. Cut in half lengthwise and squeeze out paste.

Fall Medley
of Sweet Potatoes

This is a wonderful side dish and more! Use it as a filling for baked acorn squash or as a topping for corncakes or buckwheat pancakes.

Serves 4-8

Add to a large stock pot, over medium heat:

3-4 tbsps.	OIL, Corn or Vegetable
1/2 cup	ORANGE JUICE
1/4 cup	ONION, chopped
4	SWEET POTATOES, peeled & cut into bite size pieces

Stir, bring to a boil.

Lower heat and cover. Simmer for about 15 minutes, or until potatoes are tender, stirring occasionally.

Add:

4	APPLES, cored and cut up {peeling - optional}
1 cup	DARK RAISINS
1 cup	DRIED FRUITS - peaches, apricots, cherries, etc.
1/4 cup	DARK RUM
1/2 cup	BROWN SUGAR
1 tbsp.	MOLASSES or Sorghum
2 tsps.	PIE SPICE
2 tsps.	LEMON JUICE

Simmer, stirring occasionally until apples are tender, about 15 to 25 minutes.

Serve hot.

Thanksgiving is a perfect backdrop for these very special sweet potatoes. Serve in a casserole dish topped with chopped nuts.

93

Baked Sweet Potatoes with Cranberries

This is a wonderful fall dish. It's perfect for Thanksgiving, Christmas, New Year's or anytime in between.

Serves 6-8

Add to a lightly oiled 13" by 9" baking pan:

    6   SWEET POTATOES: cooked, peeled & sliced

Layer in baking pan.

Top with:

    12 oz. pkg. Fresh CRANBERRIES, sorted, washed & drained

Option: Slice up a cored, unpeeled apple and nestle slices in the cranberries.

Sprinkle with:

1/3 cup	BROWN SUGAR
1 tbsp.	PIE SPICE
1/4 tsp.	CARDAMOM
	SALT to taste

Drizzle with:

1/2 cup	ORANGE JUICE
1/4 cup	MAPLE SYRUP or Pancake Syrup
2 tsps.	MOLASSES or Sorghum
1-4 tbsps.	BUTTER - melted
	[Use the amount that suits your dietary concerns or omit completely.]

Cover and bake at 375° F. for about 30-40 minutes or until cranberries are bubbly.

Serve warm.

This can be assembled ahead of time and refrigerated in which case you will need to increase the baking time.

Sauerkraut & Cranberries

This is a dish that combines the slight saltiness of sauerkraut with the slight tartness of cranberries with a bit of brown sugar for sweetness.

Serves 6-8

Layer in a lightly oiled baking dish:

1 can	SAUERKRAUT, 2 lb or 4 cups, rinsed and drained
12-16 oz.	Fresh CRANBERRIES, sorted, washed and drained

Sprinkle with:

1 tsp.	CARAWAY SEED
1/4 cup	BROWN SUGAR
	PEPPER to taste

Dot with:

1-3 tbsps.	Butter - [Use the amount that suits your dietary concerns or omit completely.]

Bake covered at 350°F. for 30-40 minutes until cranberries are bubbly.

Serve hot.

It is a nice dish to serve for fall and winter. Even humble sauerkraut is made festive with the addition of cranberries.

Serve with a drizzle of honey.

Judy's Acorn Squash
A Real Kid Pleaser!

This is very simple, so put away the measuring spoons.
Use a sprinkle of this and a dollop of that.
Kids will have fun making their own.

Thank you Judy Swindle!

Cut ACORN SQUASH in half

Remove seeds.

Fill hollow with APPLESAUCE.

Sprinkle with BROWN SUGAR, CINNAMON
and a pinch of SALT

Dot with BUTTER (optional)

Place in baking pan with 1/2 inch of water
in the bottom.

Cover and bake at 375°F. for 30-45 minutes
or until easily pierced with a fork.

This makes a great side dish.

Don't forget breakfast too!
Sprinkle with granola and a dollop of yogurt.

Fried Plantains

Plantains are a Caribbean side dish that would be the equivalent of potatoes in the States.

Serves 4-6

4 PLANTAINS
Peel & cut crosswise in half.
Then cut each half into 4 pieces.

Fry until golden in
3-4 tablespoons VEGETABLE OIL.

Drain on paper towels.

Season with SALT & PEPPER
&
Serve immediately

Fried Sweet Potatoes

Follow the above recipe slicing each half into 1/4" thick slices.

After frying, kids may like these sprinkled with sugar and cinnamon.

*Either of these can be served with "Picadello, a Caribbean
Beef Hash", p. 82. {Recipe in "Main Dishes"}*

Or serve as a side dish in place of potatoes or rice.

White Rice
Caribbean Style

*In the Caribbean this is traditionally served
with Black Beans as a side dish.*

Serves 6-8

Add to a medium sauce pan:

4 tbsps.	OLIVE OIL or Butter
1 medium	ONION, finely chopped
1 clove	GARLIC, minced

Sauté until onions are tender.

Add:

2 cups	Long Grain White RICE (not cooked)

Cook, stirring constantly, until butter or oil is absorbed.

Add:

4 cups	CHICKEN STOCK, fresh or canned
	Vegetable Stock can also be used
1/4 tsp.	Dried THYME
1-2 cups	MUSHROOMS, sliced {optional}
	SALT & PEPPER to taste

Bring to boil, cover and reduce heat to low.

Simmer for 20-30 minutes or until all the liquid is absorbed and the rice is tender.
If the liquid is absorbed, but the rice is not cooked, add more broth as needed.

Garnish with chopped parsley, chives or green onions.

Serve as side dish with "Black Beans Caribbean Style", p. 99

Black Beans
Caribbean Style

A little taste of the islands.
These are delicious on top of Nachos too.

Serves 6-8

Add to a medium sauce pan:

2 1/4 cups	Dried BLACK BEANS, sorted and washed
4 cups	Chicken or Vegetable STOCK - fresh or canned
	Enough water to cover beans by 3"
1/2-1 tsp.	Salt

Bring to a boil. Turn off heat. Cover and let sit for an hour for beans to soften. Bring back to a boil and then reduce heat. Simmer 11/2-2 hours or until tender. Add more water if necessary. Beans should be covered in liquid throughout cooking.
Drain.

Note: you can use 5-6 cups canned black beans, drained. Omit the above procedure and continue with the following.

Add to a large sauté pan:

3 tbsps.	OLIVE OIL
2 medium	ONIONS, finely chopped
2 cloves	GARLIC, minced
1	GREEN BELL PEPPER, seeded & chopped
1	RED PEPPER, seeded & chopped

Sauté until onions and peppers are tender, about 15-20 minutes.

Add:

3 medium	TOMATOES, chopped
1	BAY LEAF
	The drained BLACK BEANS
	SALT, PEPPER & HOT SAUCE to taste

Cover and simmer 15 minutes.

Serve hot as a side dish with "White Rice Caribbean Style", p. 98,
or with "Jamaican Style Polenta" p. 100. Also in a checkerboard pattern, p. 100.

Jamaican Style Polenta

Also referred to as Coo-coo or Fungi, this is grits with the addition of okra.
This recipe is spiced up a bit.

Serves 4-6

In a sauce pan, bring to a rolling boil:

2 cups	CHICKEN STOCK, fresh or canned
1 cup	Fresh OKRA, sliced 1/4" thick
4 tbsps.	BUTTER
2 tbsps.	GREEN ONIONS, minced
1 clove	GARLIC, minced
1/2 tsp.	SALT
1/4 tsp.	CAYENNE

While liquid is boiling, add in thin stream, whisking constantly:

1 cup	CORN MEAL

Bring back to boil. Stir until thickened, about 15 or more minutes.
Polenta burns easily, so be sure to stir constantly.
Caution when stirring polenta. When it boils, it spurts at times so, wear long sleeves to avoid getting burned.
Remove from heat. Cover.
Let it sit for about 10 minutes.
Transfer the mixture onto a heated, lightly buttered or oiled serving plate. Shape it into a round cake, about 1" thick.
Optional: Spread the top with butter. Serve immediately.
For individual servings:
    Oil or butter a small bowl, fill it with the mixture.
    Toss it around until it is smooth all over.
    Dump it onto a serving dish or individual plates.

This can be surrounded by "Black Beans Caribbean Style", for a dramatic presentaion. {See recipe on preceding recipe page.}

Checkerboard "Jamaican Style Polenta" & "Black Beans Caribbean Style"

(See Photo)

Make the above polenta. Pour into oiled 8"x*8 or 9"x9" microwavable dish. Set aside. Let cool until polenta is firm. Cut out 4 squares in a checkerboard pattern. Fill in empty squares with some of the "Black Beans Caribbean Style" from the preceding page.

Heat in microwave to serve warm.

Basic Polenta

Polenta is originally peasant dish of corn meal made into a mush, much like American grits. This is the way my Nona, from the 'Old Country' used to make it. She would always slice it with a sturdy thread, sliding it under the unmolded polenta, then pulling it up to cut it.

Serves 4-6

In a sauce pan, bring to a rolling boil:

4 cups	WATER
1/2 tsp.	SALT

While water is boiling, add in thin stream, whisking constantly:

2 cups	CORN MEAL

Bring back to a boil. Stir until thickened, about 15 or more minutes.
Polenta burns easily, so be sure to stir constantly.
Caution when stirring polenta. When it boils, it spurts at times so, wear long sleeves to avoid getting burned.

Let it sit for about 10-15 minutes to let it finish cooking.
Transfer to an oiled or buttered bowl.
Let it set for another few minutes until firm. Unmold onto platter or cutting board.
To serve. cut into slices and top with one of your favorite sauces.

Polenta Variations

Use chicken, beef or vegetable stock instead of water.

Reduce the amount of liquid and substitute the amount for cream.

Add some of any of the following during cooking:
Butter
Extra Virgin Olive Oil
Fresh or Dried Herbs
Grated Cheese
Chopped, drained Spinach
Chopped Chives or Green Onions
Chopped Olives or a Tapenades
Chopped Sundried Tomatoes

Alex's Country White Beans

with Roasted Garlic, Olives and Sundried Tomatoes

These white beans make a beautiful presentation of color and texture. It goes perfect with lamb, veal, fish or foul.

The extra virgin olive oil gives this dish its most distinctive flavor, so be sure to buy a quality oil.

Serves 6-8

Add to a large sauté pan:

4 tbsps.	EXTRA VIRGIN OLIVE OIL
1 large	ONION, chopped
1 head	Roasted GARLIC (see below)
1/2 cup	Gourmet Black OLIVES, sliced

Sauté until onions are tender.

Add:

1/2 cup	SUNDRIED TOMATOES
1/4 cup	VERMOUTH
1 tsp.	Dried THYME
1/2 tsp.	Dried ROSEMARY
4 cups	WHITE BEANS, canned and drained (If you want to cook the beans, and need to know how, follow package directions or see *"Black Beans Caribbean Style"* see page 99, in this section. Follow the first part of the recipe.) SALT & PEPPER to taste

Stir together and cook until beans are heated through.

Serve warm. Garnish with chopped parsley, chives or kale.

Roasted Garlic

Roast heads of garlic in a 375° F. oven for about 45-60 minutes or until tender. When done, let cool. Cut in half lengthwise and squeeze out paste.

Thymely Succotash

*Almost forgotten, Succotash is one of the original
"Comfort Foods". So, warm your soul with this version
and think of simpler 'thymes'.*

Servers 4-6

Add to a lightly oiled 8" by 10" baking dish:

3 cups	Fresh or frozen SWEET CORN - cut off the cobb
3 cups	Fresh or frozen LIMA BEANS
1 cup	GREEN BELL PEPPER, cut up
1 tbsp.	THYME, dry
4 tbsps.	BUTTER - more or less depending on how rich you want it
1/2 cup	HALF & HALF or Heavy Cream
1/4 cup	DRY VERMOUTH
	SALT & PEPPER to taste

Stir until mixed. Smooth out and cover.

Bake at 350°F for about 30- 40 minutes or until bubbly.

Serve hot.

*This can be made up 1 or 2 days in advance. Keep refrigerated.
Before baking, stir well and smooth out the mixture so it cooks evenly.
Cover and you may need to increase baking time for 15-30 minutes.*

*For energy efficiency, remove the succotash from the refrigerator a few hours before
baking. This will bring it to room temperature and does not increase your baking
time as much.*

DESSERTS

Life is short.

Enjoy!

And remember,
a great dessert makes
for a memorable meal.

Red Hot Chocolate Pie

*This is truly an addiction. It is a rich, custardy chocolate pie with the
addition of red hot pepper. Do you LOVE Chocolate?
And do you LOVE hot, spicy food? Well, guess what?
You've got it all right here!*

*If you are big on chocolate, but not on "hot", just eliminate the red chili
pepper flakes.*

Serves 1 or 10 if you want to share

Preheat oven to 375⁰ F.

Add to medium size microwaveable bowl:

8 oz.	Semisweet CHOCOLATE CHIPS
2 tbsps.	BUTTER

Microwave until chocolate is melted. Stir until thoroughly mixed.

Stir in:

2 cups	EVAPORATED MILK or Heavy Cream
1 cup	SUGAR
1 tbsp.	CORNSTARCH
1/4 tsp.	SALT
2	EGGS
1 1/2 tsp.	RUM EXTRACT
1/2 tsp.	VANILLA EXTRACT
1/2-1 tsp.	RED CHILI PEPPER FLAKES - more or less depending on your taste.

Using an electric mixer, mix until well combined or put it into a blender and blend well.

Pour into unbaked 9" pie shell. It will be liquidy.

Optioal: Sprinkle the top with desired amount of coarsely chopped pecans. Coconut is good also.

Bake in preheated 375° F oven for about 45 minutes.

The center will not be too firm. It will firm up as it cools.

Note: While the pie is baking, it separates into a chocolate top layer and a creamy custard bottom layer.

Refrigerate for a few hours or overnight before serving.

This pie is very rich, so you can cut it into smaller pieces than usual.

Panozzo Apple Cobbler

I like to make this in the fall when new crop apples are in season and flavors are at their peak. It is great served warm with ice cream.

Serves 6-8

Apple Filling

Add to a medium mixing bowl:

5 cups	APPLES, cut up - unpeeled
1 cup	SUGAR
2 tbsps.	FLOUR
1 tbsp.	BUTTER, softened
1 tsp.	VANILLA EXTRACT
1 tsp.	CINNAMON or Pie Spice
1 tsp.	MOLASSES or Sorghum
1/4 tsp.	SALT

Mix together.

Transfer to lightly oiled 9" by 9" baking dish.

Set aside while making Cobbler Topping.

You can substitute other fruits for apples or mix 'em up! When using other fruits such as berries and peaches, substitute lemon juice for the molasses.

Cobbler Topping

Preheat oven to 375° F.

Add to a medium mixing bowl:

1/2 cup	FLOUR
1/2 cup	SUGAR
1	EGG, beaten
2 tbsps.	BUTTER, melted - or corn oil
1/2 tsp.	BAKING POWDER
1/2 tsp.	CINNAMON or Pie Spice
1/4 tsp.	SALT

Stir together until thoroughly mixed. Batter should be thick.

Drop batter on top of apples into about 9 portions, spacing evenly.

Bake in a preheated oven at 375°F for 35-40 minutes or until apples are bubbly and topping is lightly browned.

Serve warm with ice cream, drizzling some of the sauce from the cobbler over it.

Rhubarb Cake with Strawberry Sauce

When rhubarb is in season, you'll find it fresh and piled high in roadside farm stands. Take advantage of this by trying out this delicious, moist cake.

Serves 4-6

Add to a food processor:

2 cups	RHUBARB, cut up
1 1/2 cups	SUGAR

Process just until coarse. Not too fine. Transfer to a mixing bowl. Allow mixture to sit for 10 to 15 minutes so the rhubarb has time to juice up.

Add to the mixing bowl with the RHUBARB MIXTURE:

1	EGG, beaten
2 tbsps.	OIL or melted Butter
1 cup	FLOUR
1 tsp.	BAKING SODA
2 tsps.	ORANGE PEEL, grated
1/2 tsp.	ANISE EXTRACT
1/2 tsp.	CINNAMON
1/4 tsp.	Each: CARDAMOM and ALLSPICE

Mix until well blended. Pour into oiled 9" by 9" baking pan.

Bake in preheated oven at 350°F for 30-40 minutes,

or until center springs back when lightly touched.

Serve warm with "Strawberry Sauce".

Strawberry Sauce

Add to a medium saucepan:

2 cups	Pureed STRAWBERRIES
1 cup	SUGAR
11/2 tbsps.	Cornstarch
1/2 tsp.	Grated ORANGE PEEL

Stir together and cook over medium heat until bubbly and thickened. Remove from heat.

This also makes a great topping for ice cream, cheesecake, pancakes and French toast. For crepes and omelettes, use this filling along with cream cheese and sprinkle with powered sugar.

Old Fashion Chocolate Sheet Cake

A truly wonderful chocolate cake with a thick, creamy fudge frosting. It is reminiscent of simpler times. Great for picnics, office parties and after school treats. Watch how quickly it is devoured by kids, teens and adults.

Serves 8-15

Preheat oven to 375⁰ F.

To a 6-8 quart pan, over medium heat, add:

1/2 cup	BUTTER (1 stick)	1 cup	COFFEE or Water
1/2 cup	CORN OIL	6 tbsps.	COCOA

Stir to a smooth consistency while bringing to a boil. Remove from heat.

Add:

1/2 cup	SOUR CREAM or Buttermilk
1 tsp.	VANILLA

Stir until well mixed.

Add:

2 cups	FLOUR	1 tsp.	CINNAMON
2 cups	SUGAR	1/4 tsp.	SALT
1 tsp.	BAKING SODA	2	EGGS -beaten

Stir until well mixed.

Pour into greased 15"x10"x1" baking pan or 11"x17"x1"

Bake in 375⁰ F. oven for about 20 minutes or until firm to the touch.

While cake is baking, make the frosting.

Fudge Frosting

To a 6-8 quart pan, over medium heat, add:

1/2 cup	BUTTER
6 tbsps.	MILK
6 tbsps.	COCOA

Stir to smooth consistency while bringing to a boil. Remove from heat.

Beat in:

1 lb.	POWERED SUGAR	1 tsp.	VANILLA

Beat until smooth. (Optional: add 1/2-1 cup chopped nuts.) Pour over warm cake and spread evenly. Allow cake to cool before cutting.

Create A Cheesecake

This is a No-Fail basic cheesecake. One that you can depend on to always be creamy, rich and delicious. Rob Smith made these for Panozzo's Cafe with much success.

Sometimes it is nice to use a traditional recipe. It is like having an old friend at your table.

Serves 1 or 8 if you want to share

Add to a mixing bowl:

3	8 oz. Packages CREAM CHEESE
2	EGGS, beaten
3/4 cup	SUGAR
1 tsp.	VANILLA EXTRACT

Mix well until smooth and creamy.

Pour carefully into prepared crumb crust. See below for suggestions.

Bake in preheated 350°F for 25-30 minutes.

Edges should be barely browned. Chill before serving.

Variations

* To the batter add any or combinations of the following:
dried cherries, chocolate chips, butterscotch chips, nuts, pralines.

* Top with any of the following:
fresh fruit, fruit purees, fruit sauces, caramel sauce,
chocolate sauce spiked with a favorite liqueur.

Crumb Crusts

Try using different types of crumbs like, biscotti, chocolate cookies, ginger snaps, etc. You can add a few ground nuts or coconut too.

Basic Crumb Recipe: Combine 11/4 cups fine crumbs, 1/4 cup sugar and 6 tablespoons of melted butter or margarine. Mix well. Press firmly into 9" pie plate. Refrigerate for 20-30 minutes before filling.

Perfumed Fresh Fruit

This can be served any time of the year. Use fruits that are in season for optimum flavor.   A plus to this dessert is that you never have to worry about fat grams.

Figure 1 - 1 1/2 cups of fresh fruit per person.

Into a bowl, cut up FRUIT into chunks.

Drizzle with a bit of HONEY.

Sprinkle with a little SUGAR.

Sprinkle with ROSE WATER or ORANGE BLOSSOM WATER.
(These waters impart a strong flavor, so use them sparingly.)

Try a little, taste it, then add more of what you would like.

Optional: A grate or two of FRESH GINGER.

Toss and refrigerate until serving.

Transfer to a glass bowl or nice serving container.

Garnish with flower blossoms, lemon zests or orange wedges.

Fresh fruit can be served at any time; as an appetizer, side dish, dessert or as separate course after dessert.

When I am entertaining a crowd, I always have fresh fruit out for appetizers and again at the end of the meal. It may seem redundant but it always disappears!

Full House Cookies

These are not just cookies, they are food.
You can put them in the category of a breakfast bar or a nutritious between meal snack. They are energy on the go!

This recipe makes a generous batch, so bake what you need and refrigerate or freeze the rest of the dough.

Add to a large mixing bowl:

2 cups	HONEY
1 cup	BROWN SUGAR, firmly packed
1 cup	OIL
3 cups	PEANUT BUTTER
4	EGGS, beaten

Mix together until well combined.

Add:

3 cups	FLOUR - white or whole wheat
4 cups	OATMEAL
1 tbsp.	BAKING POWDER
1 cup	RAISINS, dried Cherries or Cranberries
3	APPLES, chopped - not peeled
1 cup	NUTS, chopped
1 cup	SUNFLOWER SEEDS
1/2 tsp.	SALT

Mix until well combined. Batter should be thick.

Preheat oven to 325⁰F.

Drop mixture by tablespoons onto oiled cookie sheets, keeping them 1" apart.

Wet fingertips and lightly press down cookie dough to flatten them down a little.

Bake at 325⁰F. until cookies are lightly browned, 12-18 minutes.

Let cookies cool for 2-3 minutes on cookie sheets, then loosen with a spatula.

Let them cool on cookie sheets or on wire racks.

Store any remaining dough in an air tight container or wrap tightly in 2 layers of plastic wrap. Refrigerate. Dough will keep for up to 7 days. When baking cold dough, you may need to add a few more minutes of baking time. Dough can also be frozen. Thaw before baking and be sure to preheat oven.

Panozzo's Chocolate Chip Cookies

A Panozzo's Cafe house favorite! For my friend, Paulette Zucherman whose sweet tooth makes her a connoisseur of all things decadent.

Makes about 2 dozen.

Add to a large mixing bowl:

1 cup	BUTTER, softened
1 cup	SUGAR
1/2 cup	BROWN SUGAR
2	EGGS, beaten
1 tsp.	VANILLA EXTRACT
1/2 tsp.	ALMOND EXTRACT

Mix until smooth and creamy.

Add:

2 1/2 cups	FLOUR
1 cup	OATMEAL
1 tsp.	BAKING POWDER
1/2 tsp.	SALT
1 tbsp.	MOLASSES, optional
1 cup or more	SEMISWEET CHOCOLATE CHIPS
1 cup or more	NUTS, chopped

Note: If you don't want to use nuts, add a few more chocolate chips.

Mix until well combined. Batter should be thick.

Preheat oven to 325°F.

Drop mixture by tablespoons onto oiled cookie sheets, keeping them 1" apart.

Wet fingertips and lightly press down cookie dough to flatten them down a little.

Bake at 325°F. until cookies are lightly browned, 12-18 minutes.

Let cookies cool for 2-3 minutes on cookie sheets, then loosen with a spatula.

Let them cool on cookie sheets or on wire racks.

Store in air tight containers to preserve freshness.

To make large, oversized cookies, use an ice cream scoop instead of a tablespoon.

Cafe Apple Pie

This is not just any apple pie. It is definitely one that your family and guests will remember. This recipe uses grated apples which helps in keeping the pie dense and the top crust from collasping.

Makes one 9" double crusted pie

Prepare **half** the recipe for *"No Fail Oil Pie Crust"* on the following page, or use frozen prepared crusts. You will need 2 pastries for 1 double crust pie.

Line one 9" pie plates with pastry. Preheat oven to 375⁰ F.

Grate:

    4 medium   APPLES, cored and cut up in to small chunks (no need to peel)

Put in mixing bowl.

Add to apples in mixing bowl:

1/2 cup	BROWN SUGAR, packed
3 tbsps.	FLOUR (slightly heaping)
1 tbsp.	LEMON JUICE
1 1/2 tsp.	PIE SPICE or Cinnamon
1/2 tsp.	VANILLA
1/8 tsp.	SALT

Mix together.

Add:

1/2 cup	APPLE CIDER or Apple Juice
1/2 cup	RAISINS or chopped Dates
3 tbsps.	BUTTER, melted

Mix well. Immediately transfer to unbaked pie shell. Spread evenly. Do not let mixture sit or it will juice up too much.

Dampen edges of bottom crust with water or milk so the top crust will adhere.

Put on top crust. Cut slits for steam to escape. Crimp edges. Brush with milk and sprinkle with additional sugar. Place on baking sheet to prevent spills.

Bake at 375° F for 35-45 minutes, until golden brown and juices are bubbly and have thickened. Let cool completely before slicing.

Cutting the pie before it has cooled will result in having to deal with a runny pie. If you can't wait, serve portions in a bowl with ice cream. Yum!

"No Fail" Oil Pie Crust

*My mother, Rose Panozzo, taught me how to make this pie crust
when I was a little girl. It has never failed me. Thanks Mom!*

*Once you've tried it, you will never go back to those pain staking doughs,
nor will you be tempted by the commercially prepared ones.*

Makes 2 double crusts

Add to a medium mixing bowl:

4 cups	FLOUR, leveled off
1 cup	OIL, Vegetable or Corn
1/2 cup	MILK
2 tbsps.	SUGAR
Pinch	SALT

Mix until combined. Do not overmix. (If dough is dry and crumbly, add a bit more oil.)

Divide into 4 portions. Pat them down to flatten.

Roll out each portion between two sheets of wax paper.

You may need to remove the paper occasionally to adjust it during rolling.

Remove the top sheet of wax paper, holding on to the bottom paper and pie crust.

Pick it up by the remaining wax paper, holding on to the exposed pie crust.

Carefully flip crust onto the center of a pie pan.

The remaining wax paper should now be on top. Gently remove the remaining wax paper, then fit crust into pie plate.

Add desired pie filling. Repeat the process for the top crust.

Before applying top crust, moisten the edges of the bottom crust with water or milk so as to seal them together.

Crimp edges and cut off surplus dough with a knife. Cut slits in top crust for vents. Brush with milk and sprinkle with sugar, cinnamon or crushed nuts.

Repeat entire process for second pie.

115

Blackberry-Lemon Pie

It's nice to find fresh blackberries in season, but frozen work well too. This is an old fashion favorite with a lemony twist. Your picnic will be remembered with this pie as its finale.

Makes two 9" pies

Prepare recipe for *"No Fail Oil Pie Crust"* on preceding page (p. 115), or use frozen prepared crusts. You will need 4 pastries for 2 double crust pies.

Line two 9" pie plates with pastry. Preheat oven to 400⁰ F.

Add to large mixing bowl:

8 cups	BLACKBERRIES, fresh or frozen (do not thaw)
2 cups	SUGAR (you can use less sugar if you like)
7 tbsps.	FLOUR
2 tsp.	Grated LEMON PEEL
1/2 tsp.	CINNAMON or Nutmeg
1/8 tsp.	SALT (a pinch will do)

Mix until combined.

Pour immediately into 2 pie crusts dividing and spreading evenly.

Do not let mixture sit or it will juice up too much.

Sprinkle <u>each</u> with:

1 tbsp.	LEMON JUICE

Dot <u>each</u> with:

1 tbsp.	BUTTER

Dampen edges of bottom crust with water or milk so the top crust will adhere.

Put on top crust. Cut slits for steam to escape. Crimp edges. Brush with milk and sprinkle with additional sugar. Place on baking sheet to prevent spills.

Bake at 400° F for 35-45 minutes, until golden brown and juices are bubbly and have thickened.

Let cool completely before slicing.
Cutting the pie before it has cooled will result in having to deal with a runny pie. If you can't wait, serve portions in a bowl with ice cream. Yum!

Strawberry Trifle

A trifle is a "cake in a bowl" using a "trifle" of this and a "trifle" of that. I wanted to include this since it is easy and beautiful. It is much quicker than decorating a cake, visually appealing, easy to transport and when it comes to concocting one, anything goes!

Here is one version, but use your imagination to create your own.

Assemble the following:

2 baked	YELLOW CAKE LAYERS, 8" or 9"
1 jar	RASPBERRY JAM, heated so it is pourable
2 3.4 oz. boxes	Instant VANILLA PUDDING, prepared or Lemon Pudding or 1-2 cans Lemon Pie filling
2 pints	STRAWBERRIES, sliced
1 lg container	WHIPPED TOPPING or 2 cartons Heavy Cream- whipped cream

In a tall 8" or 9" glass bowl :

Place 1 cake layer

Spread with 1/2 jar jam

Spread with 1/2 of pudding or lemon filling

Top with 1/2 of sliced strawberries (optioanal: add 1/2 -1 cup blueberrries)

Spread with 1/2 of whipped topping

Repeat layers

Garnish with whole fresh strawberries.

Another option is to sprinkle the cake layers with a liqueur or dessert wine before assembling. Chocolate is a nice addition too.

The basics are layering cake (boxed, pound, angel or lady fingers) with jam, fresh fruit, whipped cream and custard. So, let the seasons or your taste buds be your guide. Make it colorful and have fun!

Use recipes as only a
guideline.

Read them, study them,
then create your own.

And if it doesn't turn out?
Rename it.

It works for me!

**I
N
D
E
X**

INDEX